REGRETS ON AN AFRICAN RIVER AND OTHER ADVENTURES

REGRETS ON AN AFRICAN RIVER AND OTHER ADVENTURES

JEFF SCOGGINS

Pacific Press®
Publishing Association
Nampa, Idaho | www.pacificpress.com

Copyright © 2019 by Pacific Press® Publishing Association
Printed in the United States of America
All rights reserved

The author assumes full responsibility for the accuracy of all facts and quotations as cited in this book.

Unless otherwise noted, Scripture quotations are from THE HOLY BIBLE, NEW INTER-NATIONAL VERSION®. Copyright © 1973, 1978, 1984, 2011 by Biblica, Inc.® Used by permission. All rights reserved worldwide.

Scripture marked NKJV is taken from the New King James Version®. Copyright © 1982 by Thomas Nelson. Used by permission. All rights reserved.

You can obtain additional copies of this book by calling toll-free 1-800-765-6955 or by visiting http://www.adventistbookcenter.com.

ISBN: 978-0-8163-6606-4

November 2019

Contents

Preface

Prepare for mental whiplash. You see, these are stories about my life, and my life has been experienced all over the world. So, if you care to read my stories, you will find yourself leaping from country to country and topic to topic. Sorry about that, but it has been the reality of my life.

As you read this book, you are likely to get confused about the chronology of my life, so here is my history in a nutshell.

My life

I was born in 1970 in Germany while my father was serving as a medic in the army. After the military, my dad became a literature evangelist, and I grew up moving around the southern United States wherever my dad's work took us. When I was about nine years old, in 1979, my family and I moved to Beirut, Lebanon, to serve as missionaries. An active civil war was in progress there at the time.

In 1982, my family moved back to the US, and we lived in Iowa for three years, before moving to Rwanda, Africa, in 1985. From Rwanda, I flew to Maxwell Adventist Academy in Kenya for a couple of years of school, and then I did my senior year at Far Eastern Academy in Singapore, in 1988. I then moved back to the United States for college, while my family stayed in Rwanda. I attended Union College until 1992. My parents moved back to the US at that time and returned to Iowa.

My first job after college was at the General Conference, and I lived on the East Coast for the next eight or nine years. In 1996, I married my wife, and in 1999 we moved to Moscow, Russia, as missionaries, working at the Euro-Asia Division. We returned to the US in 2003, and our first son, David, was born in 2004. Our second son, Erik, arrived in 2006. I worked as a pastor in rural Minnesota for the next twelve years. In 2015, our family moved back to the East Coast, where I work for Global Mission at the General Conference.

My agenda

I have a pet peeve when it comes to reading stories: I have never appreciated reading a story only to have the author launch into a sermon at the end. On the other hand, I am a pastor, and I understand why storytellers do that. We are not merely writing stories for their entertainment value. We want others to learn something from them. And we fear that maybe they won't get it if we don't tell them. Perhaps that isn't fair to intelligent readers. Well, I have tried to strike a balance with these stories. There is, in fact, a spiritual lesson built into each one, but it's usually short, pithy, and every once in awhile, downright clever (if I do say so myself). So give it a chance.

I hope you can learn something from my stories that runs deeper than merely laughing at my ridiculous escapades. Ultimately, I hope you discover in them the reality that nothing beats living life with Jesus.

Blessings,
Jeff Scoggins

Fleeing From a Kidnapper

When I was about five years old and my brother four—we decided we were definitely old enough to make a trip into town. I don't remember how far we lived from town, but it was several miles. Our family lived near Atmore, Alabama, just above the west corner of Florida's panhandle.

My brother, Mitch, and I needed nails. We had dreamed up a grand vision of building an ark. What fun it would be to play in such a huge boat. We had trees on our property that we could cut down and saw into boards just the way they did in the *My Bible Friends* books. My dad had a hammer and saw in the shop, but we couldn't find any nails. Not straight ones anyway. We had already pounded all the nails we could find into a telephone pole.

I had a few quarters saved in an envelope, so the simple solution was to buy more nails in town. Following family worship one drizzly morning, I asked if Mitch and I could go to TG&Y to buy nails. I don't know if TG&Y exists anymore, but as far as we were concerned, that store was the premier town destination. It sold everything one could imagine. Most importantly, it had toys, and nails, we presumed.

My mom, assuming we were pretending, thought that TG&Y was probably the woodshed or pump house and gave us permission to go. My dad left for work as we busied ourselves for our very first trip to town all on our own.

Clutching my envelope of quarters, we set out. Our long, wooded driveway ended at a four-lane highway. We thought town was to the left. The road was nearly deserted, but we stayed near the tree line anyway so that every time the occasional car drove by, we could duck into the bushes and hide.

At the bottom of the hill, we came to the river, so we were forced to abandon the trees to cross the bridge. By then, the misty rain had soaked my envelope, and in the middle of the bridge, the quarters fell through the bottom, a couple of them disappearing through drain holes into the river below. I quickly gathered up the remaining coins and shoved them into my pocket. We then raced to the other side of the bridge.

As Mitch and I neared the top of the hill, we became bolder and stayed on the shoulder out of the wet grass. We still had time to take cover when we heard cars coming toward us from the other side of the hill—at least we thought we did. A pickup truck surprised us as it crested the hill. We dove for cover, but it was too late. We had been spotted. We hoped he would just drive on. Not everyone was a kidnapper, after all.

Unfortunately, this one seemed to be a kidnapper because the minute he saw us, he slammed on his brakes and pulled to the shoulder. We were perhaps a quarter mile from home by now. "Run!" I screamed to my brother. We wheeled around and sped back down the hill toward the bridge as fast as our little legs could carry us. Having a year on my brother, I easily outran him. The large, bearded man in the pickup followed us in his truck. Finally, he pulled in front of my brother, stopped, jumped out of the truck, and grabbed him.

I wanted to keep running, but I couldn't let this stranger take my brother, so I stopped. The man deposited Mitch in the seat beside him and then pulled up to me and opened the passenger door. "Get in," he ordered. I climbed into the cab, trembling.

"Where do you live?" he asked. We pointed to our driveway, which we could still see. My terror diminished as he turned into our driveway. He was taking us home. He honked as he rolled to a stop, and my mother came out of the house. I can't remember the expression on her face, and I probably couldn't describe it if I did. I just remember her profusely thanking the man over and over as we scrambled out of the truck.

Sometimes as Christians, we develop confidence in our own abilities and set off on our own. Even though we would never say it in so many words, we live as if we do not need God. We too often commence our day without asking God to accompany us, though He is eager to do so.

When the devil finds us wandering alone without God, he is never as kind as the man in the pickup. Satan is a kidnapper, and he will do all in his power to prevent you from finding your way home. He will convince you that you haven't the time to connect with God. He will argue that it makes no difference anyhow. He will assure you that just this once is no big deal, you can spend some time with God later.

Thankfully, the devil cannot force you to climb on board with him. In fact, you don't even have to run away from him. The Bible tells us that if we simply resist him, he will do the fleeing (James 4:7).

Searching for the Roots of Heaven

I must have been only six or seven years old, but I remember vividly the night I stepped outside and found my father lying on the back porch gazing into the night sky. It was a warm, southern summer night. A million crickets performed their chorus to an unbelievable audience of stars.

My dad called me over and told me to lie down beside him. I was awestruck as I stared up at the Milky Way slung through space in perfect randomness.

"You know," said my father, "if you can stare up through space long enough without blinking, eventually you will see the roots of heaven. And if you see a streak of light, that's an angel traveling through space."

I suppose he thought that I knew he was joking, but I didn't. And I lay there staring into space long after he had gone back inside. Entranced by the idea, I stared up into space with my eyes in search of heaven and angels. Several times I thought I saw angels flashing through space. What message was God delivering? What kind of beings would receive it? What was their planet like?

Eventually, though, my eyes dried, I blinked, and I had to begin my travel through space all over again. I don't remember how long I lay on the porch looking for heaven that night, but I know it wasn't the last time I tried. Neither do I remember when I finally realized I could not see the roots of heaven, that no human could see that far.

But then again, in a way, I actually did see that far.

The fact that my father believed in heaven and cared enough to teach me how to develop my own personal relationship with Jesus gave me the spiritual eyesight that enables me to see the roots of heaven every day. What had been an off-handed joke has become something of a profound thought to me.

That night long ago, and many other nights after, in my imagination I searched for the roots of heaven. Now, even today, when I see a night sky like the one I saw that night, I like to lie on my back, trying not to blink. I watch for angel flashes and search for the roots of heaven.

The Bumblebee Nest

In Portland, Tennessee, my family and half a dozen other people were out for a Sabbath afternoon walk. We were enjoying the pleasant day and the view of a shallow pond, and we kids were running around the wide-open field. I was probably about seven or eight at the time.

Before long, I noticed a pile of boards a little distance away, which beckoned for me to jump on them simply for the entertainment of it. I ran across the field and leaped through the air onto the top piece of plywood, which gave a satisfying bounce. I instantly enjoyed my new trampoline. Unfortunately, the bumblebees underneath did not enjoy it. Evidently, what I called entertainment they called home, and they stormed out to defend it, launching several squadrons at me, attacking simultaneously. I screamed the scream of the truly panicked and began to sprint across the field.

They say that aerodynamically speaking, bumblebees should not be able to fly. I don't know who "they" are who claim such nonsense, but I can testify that bumblebees not only fly well—they fly fast. Much faster than my little legs could run.

Naturally, in my hour of great need, I ran toward those who were to care for me—the grown-ups. Not surprisingly, as I neared them with my furious bumblebees in tow, the adults began to yell and wave me away. "Don't come here!" they screamed. "Go jump in the lake!" (I should keep track of the interesting situations in which I hear that phrase.)

Frantic, I dismissed their orders and continued to rocket toward them. When they realized that I was determined to involve them, they turned and fled. When I needed them most, they left me—at high speed. That is, all except one person, who quickly emerged from the group, not running away from me but toward me.

It was my father. When he reached me, he ripped off my shirt to dislodge the bees that had set up housekeeping underneath; and then he proceeded to slap at them until he drove them off, suffering a few stings himself in the process, if I recall correctly.

By the time we got to the hospital, I felt that it was sufficiently clear that I was not going to have an allergic reaction to the bee stings. Nevertheless, despite my highly vocal protests, I got stung one more time—this time by the nurse, just in case. Perhaps this is where my needle phobia began.

When I remember the way that all forsook me, except for my dad, I think of the God who has promised to do the same for us, His children. In Deuteronomy 31:8, He says, "The LORD himself goes before you and will be with you; he will never leave you nor forsake you. Do not be afraid; do not be discouraged."

The Frog-Crushing Method

I remember the time as a kid when my parents took me and my brother and sister to an outdoor play in Missouri. Before the program began, the emcee invited all the kids up to the dirt stage area. He held up a large, heavy gunnysack and said that he had a surprise for us. Every kid in the audience scrambled from their seats and down the aisles.

The emcee dropped the sack onto the dirt and scratched a large circle around it with a stick. Then he ordered us to take off our shoes and line the perimeter of the circle. "Guess what's in the sack!" he called out.

"Candy!" yelled one kid.

"Nope. Try again."

"Rocks!"

"Nope." He let us feel the bag.

"*Eeeew!* It's mushy," screamed the girls.

"Gross!" yelled the boys.

"Mud!" yelled someone.

"Wrong again."

The emcee reached down and grasped the bottom of the sack and slowly began to tip it up as expectation mounted. Whatever was inside slid toward the opening of the sack. Suddenly, with a flourish, he snatched the sack away, exposing a heap of the largest bullfrogs I had ever seen.

The kids whooped in delight as the emcee yelled, "Everyone, grab a frog!" Mine easily covered the surface of both hands. Its spindly legs hung down at least six inches. As I stood admiring my frog and comparing it to others for size, the emcee stepped out of the first circle and with his stick, drew a larger circle around the first circle.

"Listen up, everyone," he called out. "We're going to have a frog race. Your frog must start at the inside circle and hop to the outside circle. The first frog to arrive at the outside circle wins. You must encourage your frog to hop as fast as possible. You may do anything, except you may not touch your frog until the race is finished."

We lined up with our toes on the line of the inner circle facing out, positioned our frogs between our feet, and held them in place. "On your mark. Get set. Go!" yelled the emcee.

I released my frog. Everyone else's frog leaped forward as if freedom would be the prize for winning. My frog obviously knew no such prize had been promised. He didn't move. I tried coaxing him. I tried blowing on his head. I tried yelling at him. I threatened him. I began to dance around him, screaming, "Get going!"

Finally, in desperation, I jumped high into the air, supposing that a minor earthquake might awaken my frog from his apathy. I intended to land one foot on each side of the frog. Instead, I landed one foot directly on top of him. For understandable reasons, my frog never did move.

Life is built around relationships, which, in the modern world, have become based largely on trying to persuade someone else to do something we want them to do. And even though persuasion has often been corrupted toward evil purposes, the truth is that Jesus worked the same way. He identified a person's deepest need and linked what He offered to that need. The woman at the well, Nicodemus, Zacchaeus, Matthew, Peter, Mary, the rich young ruler, and many more all felt their hearts tugged by Jesus' because He understood their deepest needs.

Christians, on the other hand, while we agree that Jesus was right, often do not operate His way. We approach someone with a not-so-subtle hint—like handing them a controversial book—then we expect one of two reactions: a door slammed in our face (persecution for the sake of Christ) or immediate acceptance of all biblical truth (slap one more star on my crown). We speak highly of Christ's method of reaching people, yet we still endeavor to move the spiritually immobile, like I did my frog, by stomping squarely on their hearts and minds. Had I been as wise, I would have enticed my frog with a tasty bug instead of demands and scare tactics.

Snakes in the Grass

In Arkansas, I went fishing one day with my grandfather, known affectionately as Granddaddy to all who knew him, whether or not they were related to him. I loved riding in Granddaddy's truck. It was a 1970 (or so) two-tone green, extended-cab, full-bed pickup with an aluminum topper on the back, carpet on the dash (a later installation), and a treasure trove of possessions stuffed into every nook and cranny. Much of it was junk, and much of it, at least to me, was far from it. Particularly the firearms.

Upon arriving at the lake, we filled a cup with worms dug from rotting logs and leaves, grabbed our rods from the back of the truck, and walked to the edge of the lake. We found a break in the lake grasses and cast our lines expecting to sit and watch our bobbers. But as soon as our lines hit the water, the bobbers plunged.

"I got one! I got one!" I screamed. But the first tug indicated a very small fish. Not that this was terribly disappointing because quantity can easily make up for size from a boy's perspective—at least until he catches a large fish. But that's another story.

Catching a fish is one of the great moments in childhood, but I discovered that the moment can become even greater. The little bluegill on my line made a run into the lakeshore grass, which was his big mistake. I would have gently removed him from the hook and tossed him back into the water. Instead, as he ran from me, he apparently ran into a water snake. Perhaps it was a water moccasin, I can't remember. They were definitely in the area because Bo Bo, Granddaddy's dog, found one on the shore before we left.

Anyway, the bluegill came off my hook—but not with my help. Instead, he was assisted by the weight of a large snake that grabbed him as I reeled the unfortunate fish toward me. I pulled both fish and snake right out of the water before both fell off and splashed back into the lake. That is remarkable enough, but then Granddaddy did the same thing and caught a second snake. I threw in my worm again and instantly caught a fish, which also swam into the grass and came out again with a brand-new tail attachment.

After the third snake, Granddaddy yelled, "Wait! Don't do it again yet." Then he ran back to the truck and returned with a .22 revolver. "OK, go!" he said. I caught another snake on bluegill bait. With remarkable accuracy for the equipment he was using, Granddaddy proceeded to shoot half a dozen snakes as they hung from my fish.

In the Bible, Satan is called a serpent, and that, too, I suppose, says enough. But I'll drag out the parallel for another moment. There were two fishermen at work that day at the lake—or rather one fisherman and one fishersnake. The man was there to catch and release; the serpent was looking for dinner. In the same way, although Jesus and Satan are both fishing for people, Jesus catches in order to free while Satan catches in order to destroy. If we latch on to Jesus' "hook," the serpent is sure to grab us from behind and pull us away. But thankfully, God knows just how to deal with serpents.

How to Get Unused to War

I pressed my back up to the cold concrete wall and shivered, not from cold but fear. I huddled under my blanket in the dark room listening to the *rat-a-tat-tat* of machine guns and the shriek-boom of mortar rockets. It was my first night in a war zone. To a nine-year-old, it made no difference that I was well out of range of the battle in downtown Beirut. It was 1979, and Lebanon was embroiled in civil war—a war that would last many more years.

Earlier that day, my family had arrived in Lebanon to work as missionaries. We had moved the few belongings we carried with us on the plane into our apartment on the mission compound, which was located on a mountainside overlooking the city. Neighbors came to welcome us, and we learned about the war waging below. Their indifference to the fighting seemed odd to me. They seemed hardly to notice it.

The neighbor kids (who would become my friends) often entertained themselves searching the flat roofs of the houses for shrapnel and bullets. No one seemed uncomfortable with the situation except me. I was wary enough during that day. The night brought all sorts of nightmares. But when morning finally arrived, I realized that I had slept. The sun brought new hope, and I even looked forward to hunting shrapnel. As that second day wore on, I noticed the gunfire less and less. That evening I *oohed* and *aahed* with the others at the spectacular tracer bullets slicing their red arcs across the night sky and the occasional bright-red cloud of an exploding rocket.

That night I slept like a hibernating bear. Soon entire days slipped by when I didn't hear the noise at all, kind of like someone who lives by railroad tracks and doesn't hear the trains thunder past. I got used to war. When the fighting came too close, I casually ambled toward the bomb shelter at the rear of the group with other macho boys. I remember once when my mom woke us in the middle of the night to move to the bomb shelter, and I insisted that they go ahead. I wanted to remain in bed. War was no longer a concern to me. Indeed, I had come to enjoy it from my relatively safe perch on the mountain. When furlough time arrived three years later, I didn't want to fly back to the US for fear of missing part of the action.

Looking back, I'm astounded at how easily I became desensitized to the evil of war. And yet, incredibly, I'm not astounded about something even worse—I am desensitized to evil in general.

The first time you ever saw a murder on television you were shocked. Today the average child sees many thousands of murders on TV by the time he or she leaves elementary school, and it's considered highly desirable entertainment. Before the days of video on-demand, I have wondered how many family camping trips have been cancelled—or never planned—for fear of missing an important episode of the latest murder mystery.

The first time you took a drink of alcohol or gulped a lungful of cigarette smoke you probably choked, but now you may not even want to quit. The first time you glimpsed porn your heart pounded, but soon the soft stuff wasn't enough. We've been desensitized to evil.

John Bunyan, in his book *The Holy War*, tells the thinly veiled allegory of the city Mansoul, which came under attack. For a while its gates, the Ear Gate, the Eye Gate, the Mouth Gate, the Nose Gate, and so on, were closely guarded. So long as the gates were watched, the city stood unconquered. Unfortunately, the gates were eventually breached and Mansoul fell.

Every Christian has been conquered by evil to some extent, but all is not lost. How does a sincere Christian regain innocence and become resensitized to evil again? It's easier than you might think. Simply slam shut the gates to your soul. Be a vigilant guard of your senses.

"A good man brings good things out of the good stored up in his heart," said Jesus, "and an evil man brings evil things out of the evil stored up in his heart. For the mouth speaks what the heart is full of" (Luke 6:45).

Sleepwalking

Part of the time that we lived in Beirut, Lebanon, we lived in an apartment building in order to be close to the bomb shelter. My parents were light sleepers when we were kids, so I don't know how I managed to leave our apartment without waking them. I have no recollection whatsoever of leaving; but when I woke up, I found myself in pitch-blackness in an unknown location.

Even then, apparently, I didn't wake up completely because even though I remember what happened, I was clearly not entirely conscious. My situation didn't concern me in the least. It seemed normal or perhaps like a game. Maybe I thought I was dreaming.

I remember thinking, *I wonder if I can discover where I am without turning on the lights?* Arms outstretched before me, I took cautious steps. My movements echoed around me, so I deduced that I was in a cave or concrete room of some sort. I encountered a cold metal door on one side, concrete walls on two other sides, and stairs on the fourth side.

Eventually, I gave up, unable to discern where I was. It was time for light. Oddly, with my subconscious in control, I suppose, I walked straight to the switch and flipped on the light. Ah! Everything made perfect sense now. I knew where I was, though I was still asleep enough that I didn't question why I was there.

I found myself in the stairwell on the basement level of our apartment building. The metal door led to the bomb shelter; the stairs led to our apartment two stories up. I bounded up the stairs to our level and knocked. The apartment doors locked automatically, and for some reason I had neglected to bring my key. No one answered at first, so I knocked again.

Eventually, I heard someone on the other side of the door trying to peer through the peephole to see who was knocking at such an hour. I was short and therefore invisible. Then I heard the voice of my father. At this point my recollection gets fuzzy again, but I think the conversation went kind of like this.

"Who's there?" my father called.

"*Marhaba,*" I replied ("hello" in Arabic).

"Who is it?" my father asked again, understandably reluctant to open the door.

"*Marhaba!*" I said more loudly.

"I'm not opening the door until you tell me who you are," said my father firmly.

I yelled, "Daddy, let me in!" My voice ricocheted violently up and down the concrete stairwell.

The door flew open, and my father stood looking at me dumbfounded. "What are you doing out here?"

I don't remember my reply exactly, but I think it amounted to "Let me go back to bed." I was no more successful explaining myself the next morning, either.

You might laugh at my story, but in a manner of speaking, it isn't an uncommon story. Spiritually speaking, we are all sleepwalkers to one degree or another. Paul says, "So then, let us not be like others, who are asleep, but let us be awake and sober" (1 Thessalonians 5:6).

We are born asleep, really; but eventually most of us wake up enough to realize that we are lost in darkness. However, we aren't very awake at first because our situation doesn't seem cause for alarm. It seems normal, in fact. Oh, we may try superficially to figure out where we are, but we treat it kind of like a game. *I wonder if I can find my way without the lights.*

It's only when we finally realize that we need the light that things begin to come together. And, interestingly, we know precisely how to locate the switch. It's like it was programmed into our subconscious all along. We call out for God, and suddenly we see our way. Only it is He who is knocking and we who are reluctant to let Him in.

But I can tell you, when you do open the door, you're going to be dumbfounded at why it took you so long.

When Caution Isn't Enough

I n Beirut, Lebanon, we lived on a hill overlooking the city. Rather than gazing at the Milky Way from our front porch, we spent evenings watching tracer bullets slicing up the night sky. We tensed and waited while a rocket screamed through the air, then we jumped and gasped when the explosion came, sending fantastic fireballs into the air. I was old enough to understand death, but I also understood that most of these explosions were destroying only concrete. We always received a warning shot and a delay to allow everyone to flee to the bomb shelter before the shelling began. Casualties, while they happened too often, didn't happen as much as one might expect in such a situation.

At first, I feared the fighting, then I became used to it, and finally I couldn't sleep when it was too quiet. One of my favorite hobbies was scavenging for shrapnel, shells, and from time to time even live bullets. My collection grew to two five-gallon buckets of hardware. Among them were several clips of live M-16 and AK-47 rounds.

As I proudly showed my dad my collection one day, he spied the live rounds and promptly set them to the side. I asked why, and he said they shouldn't be mixed in with the rest and that he'd put them in an ammo box in the basement for me. Not wanting to lose track of my prize possessions, I noted carefully where he stored the bullets.

Sometime later, my friend, Bear, as he was known, and I were idly looking for some excitement. We eventually decided that our excitement must include fireworks. Not having fireworks immediately available to us, we settled on a brilliant plan to make our own out of gunpowder, which we would harvest from my personal collection of bullets.

I climbed on top of a chair and reached the shelf where the ammunition box sat. Popping it open, we chose the smallest round, an M-16, to start with. We understood that bullets were meant to explode, so we took some precautions in case that happened. Well, we took one precaution, which entailed standing out of the line of the bullet as we wrenched it into the vise and then staying out of the way as we used a hacksaw to cut through the casing.

Slowly, cautiously, we sawed the casing until the hole was large enough to break the shell in half. Victory! We had a small amount of gunpowder. More confident, we cut a second bullet. The third went a little faster. The fourth, faster still.

The fifth exploded.

When the smoke cleared, the intelligence we had exhibited in standing clear of the sharp end of the bullet quickly became apparent. Both of us were still standing. In fact, I was unscathed. Bear, on the other hand, had gunpowder pockmarks covering his face.

We stared at each other aghast, struggling to comprehend what we had just survived.

"Are you OK?" I asked Bear.

"I think so. Are you?" he said.

"I think so," I said. "Do I have gunpowder all over my face? You do."

We quickly determined that from a medical point of view this was not serious, but from another point of view, it was serious indeed. We wouldn't be able to hide our actions. First, we knelt together and thanked God that we were unhurt; then we went and told our parents.

Cutting into a bullet with a hacksaw is kind of like playing with sin. Maybe you're cautious at first, merely enjoying the temptation. Sooner or later, however, one thing is sure, sin will eventually blow up in your face. You might be able to hide it for a little while—but not forever.

My Only Birthday Party

When I turned ten, my parents asked if I would like to have a birthday party and invite all of my friends. That sounded great! A couple of hours when I could be the leader instead of the follower. My family moved a lot, so I found that I was usually following new friends around doing what they liked to do. So when the opportunity presented itself to have my friends do my bidding—and bring me gifts for the privilege—I sprang at the chance.

I waited impatiently for the day to arrive. My mom planned the meal and, without informing anyone else, I planned the activities. First, everyone would sing happy birthday to me; then I would open all of my presents. After that we would eat cake and ice cream and then we would play a game called Dare Base. I would be the captain of one of the teams. All was arranged in my own mind.

My birthday finally arrived. It was a hot August day, and the party was outside. My friends began to arrive bearing gifts. Once everyone had arrived, they sang happy birthday to me, I opened the presents, and we sat down on the grass to eat. So far so good. All was going according to my plan. But that was where my plan ended, and their plans began.

After lunch I announced, "We're going to play Dare Base now!" The response was less than enthusiastic. "It's too hot!" "No way!" "I'm not playing." Caught off guard, it took me a moment to process the fact that no one cared all that much that it was my birthday. Other than cake and presents, life was business as usual.

Someone else yelled, "Let's have a water fight!" The suggestion was met with a cheer and a scramble for the water hose and whatever containers could be scrounged.

"Wait!" I yelled. No one listened. *OK,* I thought, *it is hot. Let's have a water fight, and then once we're cooled down, we can play my game.* Everyone had a great time until I decided we were cool enough to play my way. "Let's play Dare Base now!" I yelled. The water fight continued. I yelled again.

"We don't want to play Dare Base!" someone shrieked, dousing me with water. Angry, I stomped into the house. I wouldn't play with them anymore if I couldn't do it my way.

"What's wrong?" my mom wanted to know when she saw my face. I fought to hold back the tears. "It's *my* party and no one will do what I want to do. I want to play Dare Base. It's *my* party!" I can't remember what my mom said, but I firmly announced that I never wanted to have a birthday party again.

Since then I have learned that there are three primary ways to have people do what you want them to do. You can force them (slavery or abuse), you can pay them (salary or bribery), or you can influence them. Force and pay only work when power and money are available, but the only way to lead unpaid volunteers who have the ability to walk away at any time is through influence. People will not voluntarily follow position or authority for position or authority's sake. People willingly follow only people they respect, thereby making leadership not a matter of position but a matter of character. That is why Jesus, although humbled to the rank of poverty-stricken servant, nevertheless attracted followers so loyal that the repercussions of His life still reverberate two thousand years later. Jesus did not think the position of King of kings was something to fight for (my paraphrase of Philippians 2:5, 6). Armed with nothing but the influence of His humble character, He became the Leader of a massive volunteer movement that continues to grow like a tidal wave.

Maybe you don't consider yourself a leader, so these things don't concern you. But, in fact, you are a leader. When Jesus told us to go make disciples, He was talking to everyone who would hear that command. We have been ordered by God to lead others to Christ. That makes you and me leaders. Since we can't force people to follow us, and since we don't have enough money to pay them to follow us, all we've got left is our influence.

The friends at my childhood birthday party didn't want to follow me. Perhaps it was because I tried to command and coerce them, whether they wanted to follow or not. For good reason they rebelled—while still being my friends. Good for them.

Searching for the Ark of the Covenant

D uring our years in the Middle East, my family traveled to the place many believe is Mount Nebo, where the Bible says that Moses looked into the Promised Land before he died.

Today, at the top of the rocky hill, stands a building as a memorial to Moses. Thousands and thousands of colored rocks, cut into mosaic cubes, artistically adorn the inside of the shrine. The day we visited, a stack of papers written in English lay on a small table. My dad picked up the top page, read it, and then called the rest of us over to see it.

It seemed from the narrative that two explorers had finally found the ark of the covenant, which contained the Ten Commandments during Israel's trek through the desert for forty years and beyond. The paper instructed us to look into the valley in a particular direction and locate two trees. Between those trees was a cave. There we would find the ark. The reason it was still there, the explorers explained, was because they were afraid to touch it. Evidently, they had read the story of Uzzah, whom God struck dead when he tried to steady the ark.

My dad asked us, "Would you touch it?" I figured that I probably could touch it because God's presence was no longer there. But I thought later to myself that I still wouldn't touch it, just in case I had missed something in the Bible.

All five of us, my dad, mom, brother, sister, and I, scanned the valley in vain for two trees standing together. In fact, we couldn't see a single tree in the rugged wilderness. Finally, one of us spotted a tiny black spot in the distance. Could that be a tree or two? My dad fetched the binoculars from the car. The small dot became a slightly larger dot but still inconclusive.

"Well, what do you think?" asked my dad, seizing a golden opportunity to entertain three kids for an hour or two. "Shall we see if we can drive there?" A dirt road seemed to stumble along toward that general direction. We all voted to try and piled into our faithful blue Peugeot 504.

We drove slowly, both because the rocks could easily rip out our transmission and because signs posted every hundred feet or so warned us of the consequences of straying even slightly off the road: land mines.

Our little car struggled slowly down the backside of the mountain and then across the valley. Every so often we stopped and trained the binoculars on the trees—if they were trees. But they seemed to move with us. After perhaps an hour of tedious travel, my dad apparently decided that the entertainment value of this ridiculous trip was no longer worth the wear and tear on the car. The chances that the black dot so far away was actually a tree, much less two trees with a cave in between and the ark of the covenant inside, coupled with the fact that we saw no National Geographic film crew in sight, all added up to what must be a hoax.

Admitting we had been tricked, we turned around and drove back to the top of the mountain and down the real road on the other side—the one with no large rocks and no land-mine warnings along either side.

Remember how in the old cowboy movies good and evil were often clearly defined? The good guys wore white hats and the bad guys wore black hats. Many movies today have no such clarity. You can watch an entire film thinking the good guys are the bad guys and vice versa, and only the plot twist at the end brings it all out into the open.

The same thing will happen at the end of time. As the devil makes his counterfeits look closer and closer to the real thing, it will be difficult to know what is right and what is wrong. Our only surety is to stay on the straight and narrow road that leads to life.

What I Did Not Think About Faddy's House

"Unless you change and become like little children,
you will never enter the kingdom of heaven."
—Jesus, Matthew 18:3

D o you want to come to my house?" my friend Faddy asked me in broken English (which was far better than my broken Arabic).

"Sure," I said. After gaining my parents' permission, Faddy and I ran the length of the mission compound to the gate. We exchanged a hurried smile and wave with the elderly gate guard, Joseph, who faithfully sat at his post and took advantage of every opportunity to buy chocolate and 7up for us kids.

Faddy led the way up the hill past apartment buildings crammed together on both sides of the road, then along the back fence of the compound, then up through a small pine forest shortcut to his house. Faddy lived with his older brother and father. I didn't know anything about his mother because I never asked, and he never volunteered.

We scampered up the steps and into the open foyer of a large apartment building, our footsteps echoing in the cavernous entrance. Rather than heading for the stairwell and the building's apartments, Faddy led me to a heavy wooden door at the rear of the concrete cave. I didn't pay much attention at the time, but if I had it would have struck me as odd to go through this door. It looked like the door to a janitor's closet.

Faddy unlocked the door, and we stepped up the single step into his home. It was perhaps eight feet by twenty-five feet. Just one room. The floor was cold tile, the concrete walls painted white. A tiny window near the ceiling guarded by thick bars let only a sliver of sunlight into the room. A single bare bulb dangling from the ceiling lit the rest of the room.

Three single beds sat head to foot along the west wall and doubled as a long couch. A long counter, cupboards, and a refrigerator covered the opposite wall, leaving a two- or three-foot aisle of walking space the length of the room. The aisle ended at a wardrobe on the back wall, where clothes were stored. The stove was a two-burner tabletop device. A television occupied the far end of the counter. I don't recall a bathroom, though there may have been one by the door.

I surveyed the room without a single thought about what I had and Faddy did not have. The truth is, I probably thought about what Faddy had and I did not—a television. I wasnt jealous, I felt fortunate that I had a friend who had a television that I could watch from time to time. I determined I would visit Faddy's house at every opportunity from then on.

One time, Faddy's father came to visit my parents, and they offered him supper. Once again, the sight of how intently he ate did not strike me as odd. But as I think back, the man must have been awfully hungry. All I remember noticing about this family was that they were my friends. Faddy came to play with me most every day. He told me the story of "Ali Baba and the Forty Thieves," and other legends of *The Arabian Nights*. He came to my birthday party. Over our three-year friendship we laughed and cried, fought and made up, as kids do. He told me of his dreams to move to Australia, which he eventually did.

Since those days of childhood innocence, I have lost something special: the capacity not to judge someone based on appearances. I wish, as an adult, I still had the ability not to believe I know a person based on the size of his house or the look on his face or anything else. But that ability is gone.

Now I walk the aisles of the grocery store and effortlessly presume to know something of a person by the food in her cart or the style of her clothes, the length of his hair or the grammar of his speech, and a thousand other non-indicators.

In direct disobedience to Jesus' commands on judging others, I have acquired the capability of unconsciously stuffing people into boxes of my own invention—boxes that would not even begin to fit if I knew the person.

And that applies to the people I don't know. But what of those I do know? If I'm honest, I must admit that I'm not much better. I rarely allow someone out of their assigned box. At most, I reframe the box for them slightly and then congratulate myself on my open-mindedness. Goodness knows what would happen if I ever let them out of the cozy little home I have built for me—er, I mean, that I have built for them. Things might get out of control. Perish the thought.

Bomb Drill

Most kids are used to fire drills in school. Some are used to tornado drills. Not many have to plan for bomb attacks, though that may become part of the curriculum sooner rather than later, given the current direction of the world.

In Beirut, Lebanon, in the early 1980s, rocket attacks happened frequently. Fortunately for us, those attacks always took place down in the city rather than up on the hill where we lived overlooking the city. Because the shelling was always a distance away, we did not have bomb drills in school.

One day, though, that changed. The principal, Mr. Rose, came to our classroom (grades four to eight) and explained that today we would practice a bomb drill. Amazingly, the artillery units were usually polite enough to fire a warning rocket into the area where they were about to target and then pause for five minutes while everyone scrambled to the nearest bomb shelter. If we heard this warning shot, we were instructed to immediately dive under our desks and wait for someone to come lead us to the bomb shelter.

"Now for a practice run," said the principal, stepping out of the door. *"Shreeeek—Boom!"* he called from outside. The roomful of children giggled in delight as we dove under our desks. We waited excitedly for the next part. This was taking a lot of time away from math class! Presently the principal opened the door and shouted, "OK, let's go!" We scrambled from under our desks and followed the principal and the kids from the other rooms across the mission compound to the bomb shelter.

Sadly, the fun soon ended, and we were sent back to class. For about an hour the teacher whisked along to make up for lost time, until suddenly we heard *Shreeeek—Boom!* It was not the principal. We sat straight up and looked at the teacher. Concern flashed across the teacher's face, and she yelled, "Get under your desks!"

A minute later the door flew open and the principal yelled, "OK, let's go!" We scrambled outside, and I looked up. The sky was clear and peaceful. On the ground, though, was a different story. Girls were sobbing, and the teachers were yelling. With a wave of his arm, the principal began running toward the bomb shelter, kids in tow. The silence in the sky continued until all were safely inside the shelter. Then the firestorm broke.

Apparently, we heard later, all the hospitals in the city that treated soldiers had been bombed already. When no more hospitals were operational, the director of the hospital next to our school had announced on the radio that wounded soldiers were welcome there. The Syrians heard about the invitation and decided to destroy that hospital as well. Figuring out how to reach the target with their artillery took some trial-and-error launches, though, and our mission compound caught the brunt of it.

After the dust had cleared, we explored the damage: a large branch shredded here, a deep crater there, all the windows blown out of one home, a huge cavity in the apartment building across the street, a piece of shrapnel lying directly in front of my classroom door. Thankfully, no one that we knew of had been hurt.

That morning, had we known what the day held in store, we would have prayed for protection. Fortunately, we are promised, "Before they call I will answer; while they are still speaking I will hear" (Isaiah 65:24).

Cover-up

When my family returned from serving as missionaries in the Middle East, we temporarily moved to South Carolina. We rented a house, and for the first time in my short life I had a room to myself. It was also around this time that I discovered the public library and the wide variety of books available on subjects that interested me—subjects such as karate and judo.

I checked out every book in the library on martial arts and brought them home to my private room, where I looked at the pictures and practiced for several days. I learned the basic "horse stance" and the "forward stance" in karate. I learned how to place my weight on my back foot and move forward into a punch. I learned some sort of flying double kick and how to kick high over my head and how to curl my toes so I wouldn't break them. From my judo books I learned that if I grabbed an opponent just right, I could flip him over my head, even if he was bigger than I was.

My brother was my first victim.

"Mitch, pretend you're wrestling with me," I said. "Lock arms like this." When we had locked arms and were head to head, I explained and demonstrated at the same time that all I had to do was let go with my right arm, swing it under his right arm while still holding on to his left arm and use my back to fling him up into the air, over my head and flat onto his back. He landed with a great crash, and as he regained his wind and decided how to respond, I fled into my room and locked the door, exhilarated that the move actually worked—and worked well. However, from that day forward my brother was unwilling to serve as my sparring partner.

So I began to wish I had a punching bag, or something of the sort, for practice. Since I didn't have one, or any hope of acquiring one, I made do with what was available to me—namely, my bedroom wall. Judo is pretty useless against a wall, but for karate a wall could still be helpful.

Unfortunately, I did not know how fragile sheet rock was. I should have guessed after my first kick dented the wall slightly; but since I could barely see it, I figured small dents were harmless enough. My nearly perfected flying kick, however, sent my bare foot all the way through the wall.

Despite being shocked at my martial arts prowess, I thought clearly enough to recognize that a poster of an Egyptian mummy, which hung on my door, would look far better covering the spot where I had just smashed in the wall.

Several months later it was time for us to leave South Carolina to move to Iowa. Since we were leaving a rented house, we packed and cleaned carefully for the next occupants. I finished clearing my room and generously chose to leave a valuable donation to the next kid who would occupy my room: a superbly placed poster of an Egyptian mummy.

My father came to inspect my cleaning and right away noticed the only thing left in the room. "Jeff, are you planning to leave your poster here?"

"Yes, I think I will."

"I don't think so. Let's take it down," said my dad as he walked over and took down the poster, thereby revealing my past deed. Time had not repaired even a small part of the hole. After I truthfully confessed what had happened, my dad simply patched and painted the wall, which looked as if nothing had ever happened.

I fear that sometimes we convince ourselves that time will eventually erase our sins or that if a sin was committed ten, twenty, fifty, or ninety years ago, that God has forgotten about it. I don't find that concept in the Bible. No sin can be covered up and forgotten. If it is ever going to be erased, it must be done by confession, repentance, and forgiveness.

I Lived in Iowa and I Didn't Plant a Tree

Iowa is flat and comparatively treeless. For a Tennessee boy used to the Great Smoky Mountains and millions of trees, Iowa was a depressing place to live. While I lived in Iowa, I would have planted some trees had I thought I was going to live there long enough to enjoy them. But trees take so long to grow, and I expected to leave soon. I wanted to leave soon.

I did leave Iowa shortly after elementary school and attended high school elsewhere. As I finished my senior year, I began thinking of where to go to college. I chose Union College in Nebraska. My friends were going to more beautiful places. They couldn't understand why I wanted to go to Nebraska. The truth is, I couldn't understand myself why I decided to go to Nebraska. I had experienced Iowa. I knew better.

I feel most at home hiking the mountains, exploring the forests, and fishing the lakes. Backpacking just isn't the same when you hang your food high in a windmill out of reach of vicious cows that prowl prairie campsites. Neither could I see the appeal in dodging the local sow to fish for bluegill in her murky water hole.

Living in Nebraska did have one upside to it, I reasoned. Since everyone loves beautiful places—and in my opinion Nebraska wasn't beautiful—I felt confident of the absence of people. Being an introvert, this appealed to me. So the lack of trees notwithstanding, I chose Nebraska.

It wasn't until we crossed the Nebraska state line that I fully grasped my mistake. Waist-high wheat, interrupted by the occasional silo, greeted me with numbing endlessness. *Four years,* I thought to myself. *Can I take this for four years?* I wasn't driving, so I closed my eyes. Sleep, I hoped, would halt the brain overload I was getting from counting telephone poles.

I woke up a couple of hours later in a sort of heaven. Huge leafy trees surrounded me. Squirrels chased each other over the lush green grass, and a few students lay on blankets in the sun, their books discarded nearby. I caught a glimpse of a sign among the trees just before we turned: Union College.

I thought Union College was in Nebraska. This couldn't be Nebraska—there were trees. Big, old trees. Old enough that the man who planted them knew he wouldn't live to see this beautiful arboretum in all its glory. What kind of person dreamed that this small knoll on the endless prairie could have trees like this? Who would do it for me to enjoy?

When Jesus said "One sows and another reaps" (John 4:37), He was quoting a familiar saying of His time. Truth is a seed that grows to maturity. Sometimes we are fortunate enough to watch the Holy Spirit water and grow the seed, but more often we must be content with planting so that someone else can reap the fruits of our labor, just as we reap the fruits of those who have labored before us.

Thank you to everyone who plants a tree when you know you will never sit under its shade or enjoy its beauty. I admit, I found the Iowa prairie to be a barren place. Forgive me for living there and not planting a tree.

Wrestling My Bully

"But if you do not forgive others their sins,
your Father will not forgive your sins."
—Matthew 6:15

I don't remember how old I was when I finally exceeded a hundred pounds on the scale in the bathroom, but I do remember that I weighed in at only 111 pounds my senior year in high school. To state the obvious, I was a scrawny kid growing up. This made me prime victim material for bullies in elementary school in Iowa, one of whom was Danny. We were both in the eighth grade.

I'm not sure what Danny wanted to prove, but, evidently, he needed to prove it at the expense of the smallest kid in the class. Every day I managed to cross him in some significant way: my shadow fell on him, I raised my eyes from the ground accidentally meeting his, and so on. These crimes gave Danny all the reason he needed to challenge me to fight. For reasons that were obvious to everyone except Danny, I wasn't interested. He tried to provoke me by calling me names, shoving me, and hitting me in the shoulders. I lived in terror of Danny.

Although I was skinny as a bean pole, I must have had a little hidden wiriness because even though I didn't fancy myself a fistfighter, I held my own in wrestling matches. At evening Pathfinder meetings (a Boy Scout–style club) before the program started, we would pull out the gymnastics mats and tag-team wrestle.

Once, unfortunately for me, Danny not only showed up for a club meeting, but he was also chosen for the opposite wrestling team, which meant that I might wind up in the ring with him. We lined up on opposite sides of the mat, and the first two wrestlers began their scuffle. The lines moved as new wrestlers were tagged and the tired wrestlers moved to the rear of the line. The rules were simple. No hitting or other such non-wrestling actions, and you won by making your opponent whimper, "I give!"

I watched Danny carefully as both of us inched toward the front of our lines. My heart rate increased the more it appeared that my fears would come true. Finally, we were both next in line to enter the ring. Imagine my relief when Danny was tagged by his teammate while Ted, the biggest kid in the class and my friend, was still in the ring. At least I thought he was my friend.

When Ted saw who had been tagged, he smirked and reached out and tagged me into the ring. My jaw dropped in disbelief. Ted knew my issues with Danny, but he just whispered, "You can take him!" I didn't have a choice with so many spectators, so I stepped onto the mats. Everyone knew this was going to be an interesting match given the history of the contestants.

Rather than describe the wrestling match itself, suffice it to that say that Danny said the magic words, "I give." Everyone cheered and I jumped up triumphant. Our wresting tournaments were always conducted in good sports-manlike fashion, so I turned to shake Danny's hand as I was supposed to do. But as I turned, I met his fist full in my left eye. Blood spurted onto the mat. I was so shocked that I just stared at Danny as he screamed at me to fight him for real. I turned on my heel and walked to the bathroom to inspect my eye. Pretty noble of me, right? Unfortunately, that's where my nobility ended.

Anger replaced shock as I dabbed at my eye with a wet paper towel. When I exited the bathroom, Danny met me and did something for which I still admire him. In front of everyone he sincerely apologized to me. Unfortunately, I was so angry that I did not respond in kind. I faked an angry lunge at him, and immediately he reverted to a fighting stance and challenged me yet again. Then I walked away. *This time I had proven something*, I thought smugly.

I don't believe I consciously remembered Matthew 6:15, but subconsciously I was plagued by guilt that someone had asked my forgiveness and I had withheld it. Graciously accepting his apology in the first place would have been so much easier than what was now required of me. I had to go and apologize to him. How would he react to my apology after how I had reacted to his? Thankfully, he accepted it graciously and, amazingly, we even became friends.

It seems that there is a lot of power packed into an apology.

Mistakes

I don't think so anymore, but I once thought that one of the great advantages of living in Beirut, Lebanon, was the total absence of traffic control. Drivers paid attention to police only when it was convenient, such as when traffic became so knotted that no one could move. And knotted traffic was a regular occurrence. The worst I saw a policeman do when someone ignored him was throw a wad of keys at their car. The only uniforms anyone paid attention to were the heavily armed soldiers who commanded the frequent checkpoints.

However, chaos was not the great thing about the traffic situation. The best advantage I noticed was that drivers' licenses did not exist; therefore, anyone could drive. One time, as our family drove a deserted mountain road, a yellow sports car blew past us with a child at the wheel, craning to see through the windshield from his perch on top of phone books or pillows. We soon caught up with him as he sat stopped at a military checkpoint. The soldiers were laughing. I got out of the car with my dad to check out this marvelous thing. The soldiers asked the boy how old he was. Thinking back today, I realize that my memory must be flawed, but I distinctly remember the kid holding up five fingers. Now that I have children, I know that simply can't be right. However old he was, though, he was younger than I was. So at eleven years old, I was awestruck.

That is why, when one day, my father roared across the lawn toward me astride a brand-new motorcycle, I imagined glorious possibilities. Finally, I would drive. Incredibly, he agreed to teach me. I climbed on the back, and we drove up the hill to Middle East College's (now Middle East University's) dirt soccer field. My dad made some skid marks on the ground for me to follow, and after a little clutch and throttle instruction, I drove. It wasn't hard. I quickly gained confidence as I guided the bike around the skid marks. One mark, though, bent at a right angle, and try as I might, I couldn't follow it.

Finally, determined to corner sharply enough, I cranked the handlebar, and in so doing, I wrenched the throttle. The front wheel came up, and I quickly rocketed toward my dad and the high rock wall a few yards behind him. He yelled, "Let off the gas!" Panicked, I opened the throttle wider, and the back wheel began to bounce off the ground. I think my dad was preparing to pull me off of the bike as I flew by, but before that became necessary, I managed to bring it under control. Greatly shaken, I gladly let my dad drive home. Perhaps unfortunately, a couple of days allayed my nervousness, and I began practicing again.

About that time, I decided to attend baptismal classes at the college church up the mountain. I would drive the motorcycle there to attend classes. My dad said he would ride as I drove the first evening, and after that, I would drive myself. Rounding a curve with my dad on the back, I once again popped a wheelie. How my dad hung on at that angle, I'll never know, but he somehow managed to push forward over me and force the front wheel back to the road.

Although I could tell many more stories about learning to drive vehicles, suffice it to say I messed up a lot. But I never heard disparaging criticism from my parents. Imagine if they had lost patience or been paralyzed by the fear that I would hurt myself so that they insisted on always driving me. What if they had wanted to protect me from making mistakes—even injurious ones? By definition, learning involves doing things less than perfectly for a while. And that goes for maturing mentally as well as spiritually.

Fighting Spiritual Gravity

I was fourteen years old and gearing up to go away to boarding school. That was the only choice we had after our family moved to Africa, and I wasn't complaining. I had arrived at the age where I knew everything, so I was raring to get out on my own. Not that boarding school would give me much independence, but it had to be better than being home, where I was convinced that life was much too restricted.

We had moved to Rwanda only a month or so earlier and were heavily involved in learning Kinyarwanda, the local language. I found it much more interesting, however, to play with my new friends, who were the kids of the mission faculty at the Adventist university in Mudende. There were only a couple of boys my age and a whole passel of them slightly younger than me. I found that I enjoyed the company of the younger boys more because the older ones were into music and clothes and stuff that I found uninteresting. I much preferred climbing trees, getting dirty, learning to do handsprings, digging caves, and so on.

When the big day came for me to fly to Maxwell Adventist Academy in Kenya for school, all my friends saw me off. We said our goodbyes and promised to pick up our activities in December during Christmas vacation, a promise that I had every intention of keeping.

Boarding school was a new and different life for me. I had to learn about the school culture, much like I had to learn about the culture every time I moved to a new place. Adept at the process by now, I changed quickly to fit in. But I wasn't conscious of the changes because they were not major. I didn't think my way through the process; I simply felt my way through without understanding. Consciousness came several months later.

December arrived, and the school emptied as all the students flew to various countries where their parents were serving as missionaries. I flew to Rwanda, my mind filled with the anticipation of meeting my friends and how I would impress them with my new grown-up life. By this time, my parents had moved from the university to Kigali, where my dad was working, so I wouldn't see my friends until the weekend when we would drive to Mudende.

I prepared all week for the reunion. I carefully chose what I would wear. I consciously parted my hair in the new way I had picked up at high school. I thought about the music I would listen to with my friends. When we finally arrived at Mudende, our truck was mobbed just as I had pictured would happen. I leaped out, and my friends began talking excitedly. "Jeff, do you want to go climb trees?" "Want to practice handsprings?" "Our cave has filled in, and we need to dig it out again!"

I looked at them like they were aliens. They hadn't changed at all, but I became suddenly aware that I had changed. It had happened gradually over months, so I hadn't noticed the difference in myself and probably never would have but for the abrupt contrast of my friends. They revealed to my consciousness what had taken place in me ever so slowly and unconsciously. By the end of the weekend, I was hanging out with the older boys listening to music and wearing cool clothes and other stuff that had, a short time before, been uninteresting.

Thankfully, I eventually outgrew that stage of maturity (or immaturity) also, but that childhood memory has never left me. It has taught me that how I continue to grow and change is not completely outside of my control. The minute-to-minute decisions I make, as mundane and ordinary as they may seem, profoundly influence how I grow and change not just in character maturity but in spiritual maturity.

I long convinced myself of the existence of a neutral category—choices I could make that would not impact my spirituality either positively or negatively. But as much as I may wish for such a category, it simply does not exist.

Like it or not, we are captive to the relentless process of spiritual growth. We are either being formed into the likeness of Jesus or into the likeness of His enemy. And whatever does not draw me toward Christ actually drags me away from Him, even if I don't realize it.

Right Thing, Wrong Way

I was too young to have a driver's license, but I was getting close. Not that it mattered in Rwanda, since I'm pretty sure no one had a license back then. Driving, for a boy my age, was naturally a big deal, even if it was through a game park over dirt tracks that could hardly be called roads.

One day my dad asked me to drive our little Peugeot not through a game park but to a little shop about a mile away, mostly downhill from our house, to buy some bananas. He gave me one hundred franks, about a dollar at the time, for the bananas. My brother jumped into the passenger side, and I shoved the car into gear, pleased to drive without a parent along.

The trip down the hill went uneventfully. Buying the bananas went uneventfully. But driving back up the hill didn't go so well. Try as I might, the car simply would not drive up the hill. It would try to pull itself up the steep incline, but it lacked the power to do so. I was experienced enough with a clutch not to stall it, and I knew the trick of using the hand brake to keep from rolling backward down the hill. But the car simply refused to climb the hill. I worked the clutch back and forth, rocking the car, revving the engine, and still no luck.

After a while, I began to smell a burning odor, and then the car stopped moving altogether. I walked the mile home with a heavy heart.

My dad and I got into "The Beast," which was the name of our ancient-but-still-strong Land Cruiser. Emergency equipment, including extra gas, first aid supplies, car parts, tools, and chains, lived in "The Beast" just for such occasions.

At the car, my dad showed me that I had been using third gear instead of first gear. On a hill that steep, I had burned out the clutch.

We towed the little car home and parked it under a shade tree in our yard. The next day a mechanic who made house calls tore it apart, and in short order, he replaced the clutch. My dad still fondly recalls his three-hundred-dollar bananas. I don't remember them being all that good.

I had done the right thing, but I had done it the wrong way. I had permission to be driving. That was right. Leaving home, I had probably started in third gear, too, but I was starting downhill, so in that circumstance, it worked. I had used the brakes properly. I even worked the clutch correctly. The only problem was in the last circumstance, third gear wasn't good enough. There are wrong ways to do right things. The end does not justify the means. God not only cares about where we end up—He also cares how we get there.

"There is a way that appears to be right," said King Solomon, "but in the end it leads to death." He must have really been convinced of this because he wrote it twice (Proverbs 14:12 and 16:25).

Claiming the Name in Vain

I have been to India. If you have read the previous stories in this book, that's hardly news, since I tell stories from all over the place. So let me tell you about Bombay, known as Mumbai today. I was flying from Rwanda to Singapore, where I was to complete my senior year of high school. On the way to Singapore, I had the opportunity to experience India.

Here is my experience: People lay, squatted, stood, and milled about like piles of litter. The smell was, well, memorable. It was boring. There was nothing to see, nothing to do. I wished I had brought a book with me. I remember a lot of dirt, few places to sit, inconvenient access to restrooms, and no food. I didn't enjoy India.

Oh, did I mention I never left the airport? I had a ten-hour layover in Bombay along with thousands of other passengers. We sprawled all over the airport, jet-lagged, bored, unrested, and un-showered. The fact is, at any given time, you can find a similar scene in any of a thousand other airports around the world, including the US.

So how fair is it for me to say that I have experienced India? It's not fair at all. A brief layover in the airport is not really visiting India. And yet, if I cared to, I could probably fool most anyone who hasn't been to India into believing that I had truly experienced Bombay. Indeed, if I wish, I can even fool myself into believing that. For proof, just look at my map where I can record all the places I have visited. India is marked.

I have also marked Japan, Uganda, Ethiopia, Burundi, and Bahrain. Yes, I've been to those countries—in the airport or in some cases just the airplane. Why did I mark them when I haven't really visited those countries? Because it's cool to say I've been there. It makes people say, "Wow! You're quite the world traveler." It's fun to see the number of countries add up and compare your count to others. Call it the traveler's version of "keeping up with the Joneses."

I tell this because I sometimes think we deal in much the same way with our spiritual life. It can be convenient and satisfying to be a Christian in some parts of the world today. When we are surrounded by people who call themselves Christians, it's the agreeable thing to cast ourselves in that mold. Just ask campaigning politicians. In many arenas it's cool to say, "I got saved on August 13, 1977." It makes people say, "Wow! You're quite the committed Christian." It's fun to see how your spiritual experience compares to that of others who call themselves by the same name. Call it the spiritual version of "keeping up with the Joneses."

And even if no one can see a difference between your life before August 13, 1977, and your life after that, it's easy to fool someone who hasn't experienced Christ for himself into believing that you have. Indeed, if we wish, we can easily fool ourselves into believing it. Just look at how many of us label ourselves "Christian" but in practice, shame that name by not living it. I'm serious. If you see a bumper sticker that says "Honk if you love Jesus," you'd best not do it.

To be truly honest, we need to take a hard look at our claims of knowing Christ, and if we realize that we have only visited the airport and have not really experienced Him in a life-changing way, then perhaps we should take immediate action to either remove our Christian label or get serious about experiencing Christ in a way that actually changes us.

I don't know if the legend is true, but the story goes that Alexander the Great came upon one of his soldiers who had acted in a cowardly or disgraceful way. Alexander asked the soldier his name, and the man replied, "Alexander." To that Alexander the Great replied, "Then you better change your name or change your ways."

If you sense deep inside that you are not following Jesus as you should, then do Him the favor of not calling yourself by His name. Don't call yourself a Christian until you're ready to fully experience Him, fully yield to Him, fully commit your life to Him. Do it no matter what "the Joneses" are doing.

They Trashed My Room

I n the late '80s, freshmen at Union College had the privilege of living in a separate men's dormitory—one that could more afford the abuse that often accompanies energetic youth activities. Looking back, I see the wisdom in the policy. However, during my freshmen year that dorm was only sparsely populated, which meant that partway through the year, we were each given the option of having our own room. I took it.

One day, my friends Doug and Greg were in my room when Doug, unprovoked, stood and yanked out one of my desk drawers and dumped its contents into the middle of the floor. Then he dropped the empty drawer on top. With a wide grin, he looked for my reaction. Caught completely off guard, I just cocked my head. I didn't get the joke. But apparently, Greg did because he laughed uproariously then jumped up and pulled out another drawer and dumped it on top of the other.

Suddenly, both Doug and Greg leaped into furious action depositing all of my earthly possessions into a heap in the middle of the floor. Powerless to stop them and knowing I'd look foolish by trying, I simply watched. Eventually, I had a bright idea, so I left the room, closing the door behind me. Unfortunately, I found their doors locked, so my bright idea went nowhere. Revenge would have to wait. I walked back to my room and found my door locked.

Inside was silence. They couldn't have left the room without me seeing them.

I knocked. I called. Still silence. Eventually, I found a dean who let me into my room. The window was open. That had been their exit. The dean looked at the great pile in the middle of my room. Nothing had been left in its proper place. The dean cast a quizzical look at me then left without a word. Whether my room had needed it or not, it received a thorough reorganizing.

First Corinthians 3:16 presents an image of our bodies as a home where the Spirit of God can live. But it can become the home of a different spirit as well. We have a real enemy who enjoys nothing more than moving into our lives and making a wreck of it. One by one he pulls out the stops on our inhibitions and then tosses in small bad habits. The mess grows from there until finally, nothing is untouched. The destruction hurts our families, our friends, ourselves, and even God.

Do you sit by and just watch him do it, maybe even thinking that you'll look foolish trying to stop him? Perhaps you check out mentally and ignore what's going on, figuring you'll just clean up later. I wonder what would have happened that day if I had dropped to my knees in my room and began to ask God to stop Doug and Greg. At the very least, the look on their faces would have been priceless. Fortunately, we don't have to wonder what happens when we drop to our knees for help against Satan. He isn't confused; he's terrified. He runs. The Bible tells us, "Resist the devil, and he will flee from you" (James 4:7).

Here's a bit of advice, though, from Jesus. When you get your "home" back and sweep it clean, fill it completely with the Spirit of God (Luke 11:25, 26). Do not resist the devil defensively, resist offensively. Pray and study the Bible to fill the home of your heart with the One who will not sit idly by the next time someone tries to trash your life.

Mob Mentality

One of my roommates at Union College in Lincoln, Nebraska, was Doug Nesmith. In the late eighties or early nineties, he and I drove to the mall. We were searching for another friend by the name of Tom. We began to roam the corridors looking for Tom, but in the crowds, it soon became evident that we could be looking for quite some time.

Doug decided that in addition to looking, we needed to call for Tom, so he suddenly called out, "Tom!" He didn't yell, but he said it loudly enough to be slightly embarrassing. It's not that Doug was unaware that what he had done was embarrassing; he intended it to be embarrassing. Doug and I often sought creative ways to push the social etiquette envelope just for the shock value. Therefore, I immediately felt the need to one-up Doug's boldness.

Slightly louder than Doug, I followed suit by calling out, "Tom!" To my satisfaction, more heads turned for my call than had turned for Doug's. Doug yelled again more loudly, and then I yelled even louder. Soon, in a mall packed with shoppers, Doug and I were walking the corridors and stores yelling, "TOM!" at the top of our lungs.

An act that just minutes before would have been unthinkable, we now did with gusto. Something we would never have done alone, we did easily together. There's a sociological term for this. It's called "mob mentality."

Screaming in the mall, while a bit immature, is a harmless manifestation of mob mentality. But the same mental phenomenon frequently takes on a more sickening shape. It's how law-abiding citizens can start riots. It's how teenagers sample illegal drugs. It's how suicide bombers can strap on explosives. It's how prison guards can torture inmates. It's how terrorists can behead innocent victims. It's how entire races of people become classified as animals by other races of people. And, unfortunately, it's often the way you and I choose our path in life.

Put a dozen brains together in the right circumstances, and they can't seem to think separately. Peer pressure and mob mentality are powerful enough to make people do what they wouldn't do alone. And we can't reserve the effect for teenagers and terrorists.

In less jarring instances, mob mentality is called conformity. It happens when you get into the elevator and turn to face the door. Try stepping into an elevator someday, and don't turn around. Just look directly at everyone else.

It happens everywhere. No one builds a stilt house in suburbia. Men wear ties even though they serve no function. By nature, we conform to those around us in good and bad ways.

I've seen people temporarily reject their Christianity in a setting of unholy influences. But I've also seen people suddenly gain a Christian experience when that seems to be the cool thing to do at the moment.

In my opinion, one of the characteristics that God values most in His children is our ability to think for ourselves in spite of what is happening around us. That, I believe, is what Jesus meant when He commanded us to be in the world but not of it. Just as a ship is in the ocean but not of the ocean, so must God's people exist in the crowd while not being lost in the depths of its influence.

But what do we do with that powerful desire within us to conform? First, using God's Word as our filter, we can see where we may be tempted to conform in ways contrary to God's will. Next, using prayer as our lifeline, we ask God to do the work in us that we can't do for ourselves. Finally, we can learn to enjoy being nonconformists.

I'm never wearing a tie again.

Speaking Australian

My college roommate, Doug, was not Australian, and neither am I. Indeed, we have never been to Australia. Nonetheless, Doug and I discovered that we had a knack for speaking with an Australian accent. We spoke our new dialect so much that after a while, it became a habit, and as a result, we stumbled upon a fantastic discovery.

It happened like this. One day, as we searched for something in Walmart, we passed a store employee, a young lady. When she heard our accent, she stopped her work and asked with a big smile, "Where are you from?"

Thinking fast, I said, "We're from Barrow Creek. You've probably never heard of it."

"What country is that in?" she wanted to know.

"Australia," said Doug.

"Wow! What are you doing here?" she asked.

"We're on walkabout," I said.

"Like Crocodile Dundee? Wow! That's so cool!" she exclaimed. You can forgive her for the overreaction since, after all, it was Nebraska.

Right away, Doug and I both grasped the fact that we had stumbled upon a great gag. We drove directly to a different store. We walked past the battery aisle several times in search of a suitable store employee. Finding one, Doug walked up to her and, in his best Australian, said, "G'day, miss. Could we bother you for some information?"

She smiled broadly. "Of course!"

I said, "We're looking for some batt'ries and can't seem to find them."

"Some what?" she said.

"Batt'ries," Doug said. "You know, like to make a flashlouit work."

"Flashlouit?" she looked confused. And then, "Oh! Batteries for a flashlight?" she said with sudden understanding.

"Yeah, yeah, batt'ries for a flashlouit," we nodded.

"Sure, they are right over here," she said, guiding us to the battery aisle. On the way, she asked where we were from, and we spun the Barrow Creek lie. When we turned the corner into the battery aisle, Doug and I both stopped.

"Wow!" I said. "There are so many!"

"How do you choose?" Doug asked. After having her help us find the proper batteries and show us to the cashier, we had the cashier show us the value of each of our American coins so that we could pay the proper amount. Then we laughed all the way back to campus.

Our antics went on for most of the school year, getting more and more elaborate each time. One day, on a road trip down the interstate, we stopped at a rest area. As I waited in the car, I saw Doug exit the restrooms and strike up a conversation with a gentleman standing on the sidewalk. I knew that Doug was speaking Australian as usual, and I thought nothing of it.

Suddenly, I saw Doug's face glow red. He dropped his eyes to his feet and walked quickly to the car and slumped into the passenger side. "Let's go!" he said sheepishly.

"What happened?" I wanted to know.

"He was Australian," said Doug flatly. He didn't laugh this time, but I did.

So many people fell for our Australian farce because they didn't know what an Australian really sounded like. But to the true Australian, the deception was immediately seen for what it was: a lie.

G. K. Chesterton says, "Falsehood is never so false as when it is very nearly true."[1]

Satan has been working for thousands of years on this last great deception that will look so nearly perfect that Jesus said if it were possible, it would deceive even the very elect (Matthew 24:24). The only way you will recognize the false is if you know the True.

1. G. K. Chesterton, *The Collected Works of G. K. Chesterton*, vol. 2 (Ignatius Press: San Francisco, 1986), 473.

Sleeping Contentedly on Too-Short Benches

I had two enemies all through college. We were roommates. We spent much of our time together. We ate together, played sports together, talked together. And we played practical jokes on each other, which is why I call them enemies. They were Doug and Greg.

Practical jokes are a staple of college dormitory life, particularly for freshmen guys. The object of this "immature behavior," as some believe it to be, is to one-up the joke on the other person. In this tradition, Greg, Doug, and I relentlessly abused each other through all four years at Union College. The occasion I'm thinking of was when Greg and I removed the entire contents of Doug's room—the bed, dresser, lamps, clothes, books, and so on—and neatly arranged them in the public bathroom down the hall.

When Doug walked into his room and found only his roommate's things there, he exhibited little reaction but began wandering the hall in search of his belongings. As I recall, he was a resident assistant and, therefore, owned a master key, which he used to check each room. Eventually, he checked the bathroom. Still, with little more reaction than a laugh, he quietly removed the things he needed and left everything else in the bathroom arranged as it was.

Doug then dragged a bench only about five feet long from the hallway into his room and slept on it for the next two months without complaint. Someone else eventually cleared the bathroom, and by the end of the school year, most everything had found its way back to Doug's room piece by piece.

I can't decide if this is an especially poignant or especially ridiculous illustration of the idea that Satan takes every good thing that God has given us and rearranges it in the bathroom, so to speak. In other words, Satan continually attempts to replace the good and perfect gifts of God with corrupted versions of that gift. Just look at what he has managed to do with sex, appetite, ambition, beauty, music, pleasure, intelligence, entertainment, and even love.

However, Satan is God's archenemy, so his war against God is not really shocking. What is more shocking is that we don't seem to react at all to the cruel joke. We seem content with the new arrangement. We might rescue a few convenient things, but we basically leave Satan's arrangements intact. We indulge our appetites according to Satan's prescriptions. We allow our ambitions to clamber over people. We accept the picture of beauty as scrawny, half-clothed, and airbrushed. We learn to enjoy music that makes our hearts beat out of rhythm with God. We allow our intelligence to become a god or an excuse. We swallow the idea that love is giving us whatever we want whenever we want it. We're contentedly sleeping on too-short benches.

Regrets on an African River

The summer of 1990, before school started and after I had finished my summer job, I flew to Africa to visit my parents, who were working in Rwanda as missionaries. My cousin, Cameron, was also visiting at that time. The days were lazy, and Cameron and I were discussing how to occupy ourselves when Carl Wilkens, director of the Adventist Development and Relief Agency in Rwanda, drove up in his Isuzu Trooper. He asked if we wanted to go river rafting with him that afternoon. We were enthusiastic despite his warning that the river was infested with crocodiles and hippos. Twenty-year-olds, after all, are invincible, right?

The day was typically comfortable, so Cameron and I changed into old shorts, T-shirts, and tennis shoes. I clipped a boot knife to my belt and then filled up a liter bottle with water. We did not bring food because we expected to be home in time for supper.

Carl arrived at 1:00 P.M. with his wife, Teresa, who would drive home and then later meet us at a bridge farther downriver. Carl hefted two baseball bats and asked if we thought we should bring some anti-crocodile implements. I patted my knife and agreed that caution was good. We drove to the bridge where we planned to unload but found a group of Rwandese soldiers already there, who—despite our poor language skills—managed to communicate to us that we couldn't put in there. So we drove off-road along the river until we found a suitable spot.

Using a foot pump, we inflated two small rafts with air. Carl explained that when the motor batteries died, we would simply stash them in the other raft and float with the current. We loaded oars, a patch kit, bats, water, an electric motor, and batteries—but no life jackets that I can recall. I sank to my knees in mud as we pushed the rafts into the river. Teresa would meet us at about 5:00 P.M. at the next bridge downriver. If we arrived earlier than that, we would simply wait.

The river was the color (but not the taste) of hot chocolate, and it averaged, perhaps, fifty feet across. Soft dirt banks anywhere from three feet to twenty-five feet high gave us the feeling, at times, of floating down a small canyon. The occasional mud bar jutting out into the river provided opportunities to refill the rafts with air, which deflated at a regular rate. These mud bars also served other purposes—such as a spot for crocodiles to sun.

"Croc!" we yelled in unison as we rounded a bend in the river. It was at least twenty feet long and two feet wide, though it may have grown in size over the retellings of this story—but not by much. However big it was, nothing that size should be able to move as fast and jump as high as that crocodile did. Almost effortlessly, it leaped three to four feet in the air and dove into the water in front of us. Cameron and I grabbed the baseball bats. *"Go for the eyes,"* I remembered hearing. After a few moments, when the crocodile didn't surface, Carl yelled, "Row!" We rowed. Fast. And we didn't stop until we were far from the area.

No sooner had our heart rates slowed when we rounded another bend and yelled together, "Hippo!" I had been told that if I was given a choice between wrestling a crocodile or a hippopotamus that I should choose the crocodile. I had also been told that hippos walk under the water and then surface underneath your boat. Startled by our yelling, this hippo did indeed walk toward us into the water until she was completely submerged. "Row!" yelled Carl again, and again we dropped our bats and rowed with passion. After we slowed, Carl said, "I don't regret that we came." With brave laughs, Cameron and I agreed. We inspected the next mud bar particularly well before pulling over to reinflate and transfer our dead batteries and motor to the second raft, which we towed along behind us.

Back on the river, we soon encountered a mid-river hippo party. "We better walk around this group," advised Carl. We tied a long rope to the rafts and scrambled up the high bank. At the top, a group of Rwandese farmers greeted us. Though we didn't speak Kinyarwanda well, we managed to understand that they were questioning our intelligence level, which couldn't be too high, given what we were doing.

The farmers followed us as we pulled the rafts toward the hippos. Unfortunately, a thick stand of brush and trees growing atop the very edge of the high bank would not allow us to continue and still hold on to the rope. Not wanting to release the rafts and not being able to pull them out at this point, Carl volunteered to jump down the bank twenty feet or so and row the rafts along the bank and by the hippos. If worse came to worse, adrenaline would probably propel him back up the near-vertical incline, he reasoned.

Carl leaped over the edge, landing in the soft dirt about halfway down the bank, and then took another leap to the bottom. When the farmers realized what was happening, their excited yells communicated clearly what they thought of Carl's plan. Quickly, they snatched handfuls of rocks and began running along the river ahead of Carl, yelling and throwing rocks at the hippos. Cameron and I followed suit, and Carl paddled through safely.

By this time, we were ready for our rendezvous bridge to show itself. We expected it at every bend. We asked every farmer we passed in the fields how far to the bridge, but we never received a definitive answer. We got hungry. "I still don't regret the trip," said Carl again. And Cameron and I courageously agreed. But as the sun hung low over the hills, we decided to go easy on the little water we had left.

Then it got dark. So dark that we couldn't see the riverbanks on either side of us. Our raft was dangerously low on air, but the invisible sounds of darkness around us made us reluctant to land. Suddenly, we heard the distinctive laugh-like grunt of a hippo a short distance in front of us. Then another answered not far behind us, and then another not far to the side. It sounded as though we had floated into the middle of a large company.

"Do you think we should pray for help?" Cameron asked. Embarrassed, I gave an uncomfortable grunt. In my heart, I had the same thought, but I said, "I think we have been praying already." And the conversation died right there, on the altar of pride. I didn't want to admit weakness. The truth is, I was ashamed to pray.

"I think we had better land and try to walk out," said Carl. "I can come back on the motorcycle tomorrow to pick up our gear." Carl paused, then said, "But I still don't regret the trip." Our words agreed, but for my part, my enthusiasm was going the way of the temperature. I shivered in my wet T-shirt and shorts.

We cautiously steered our raft to the west bank, our eyes willing the darkness to reveal anything that would not appreciate being stepped on. The moon made a welcome appearance as we collapsed the rafts and hid our gear beneath a clump of riverside bushes. Carl would need to return early if he hoped to find everything before someone else did. My watch read 10:00 P.M.

We began walking south with the river, through the soft dirt of the newly hoed sweet potato fields. Before long, we happened upon a smoldering tree stump that someone had been burning out that afternoon. It wasn't warm enough to do us much good, so we trudged on. We were soon stretched out single file, one hundred yards or so apart, the distance growing; Carl in the lead, me in the middle, and Cameron in the rear. We shuffled silently, heads down, watching our feet like we were trekking through a desert. At about 11:00 P.M., I met Carl returning. "It's all swamp ahead," he said flatly. "I couldn't find a way around, and we definitely can't go through."

As Cameron caught up to us, suddenly, on the opposite side of the river, a pair of headlights cut through the night, tracing a path along a distant road. Our hopes suddenly soared, and we walked quickly to the riverbank. That road could lead us out of this situation. We stared warily at the black water swirling below us and seriously considered swimming across, but better judgment prevailed. "I guess we'll be out here for the night," said Carl. "Why don't we go back to that burning stump to see if we can start a fire?"

Back at the stump, we spied a large stack of dry grass nearby that had been cleared from a field. I grabbed an armload and threw it onto the stump. It erupted into a flame, flinging back at us a welcome burst of heat lasting all of three seconds. We threw on another load, then another, but realized that as large as the stack was, this fuel would not last long. Instead, why not crawl inside like a haystack and sleep in the pile of grass? It seemed like a good plan, but when we had carried the stack to a good spot and removed the top to bed down, it occurred to us that we were going to have to sleep close, very close— uncomfortably close. Finally, someone said, "I won't tell anyone if you won't." We agreed and drew straws for the unlucky person who would take the middle spot. The lot fell to me. We climbed in, pulled the top of the stack on top of us, and I fell asleep as someone said, "I still don't have any regrets."

About an hour later, both Carl and Cameron leaped up, grabbed a large load of grass, and threw it on the stump for the brief blaze. I groggily asked what was happening, and they chattered, "We're freezing."

"Why?" I said. "I'm toasty!" Suddenly the middle spot was the coveted one.

"Cameron is next," ordered Carl, "then me." We spent the rest of the night rotating between warmth and sleep and cold and restlessness. I suppose I have never welcomed a sunrise as I did the next morning.

As the sun burned its way over the hills, it also burned hope into us. We bounded out of our haystack, burned it, then struck off to find our boats. Our gear was untouched, but as soon as we uncovered it, we attracted a crowd of farmers who were arriving in the fields. We patched a few holes, inflated the rafts, and with no crocs or hippos in sight, we put out to open water.

At around 10:00 a.m., we heard the distinctive *chop, chop, chop* of a helicopter, and turned to see a fully armed French military gunship weaving its way down the river toward us. Carl stiffened. "Guys, please don't wave until we know they are searching for us," he said. It quickly became apparent that they were, in fact, searching for us because, as soon as they saw us, they began to circle. We waved and gave them a thumbs up. They waved back and relayed a message to our families that we had been found safe and our ETA at the bridge, which was about two kilometers farther down the river. We found out later that a friend who had several friends at the French military base in Kigali had asked them to look for us.

When we arrived at the bridge an hour later, my father, Carl's wife, and a platoon of Rwandese soldiers awaited us. My dad pulled us in and said dryly, "You think you're going home, but you're not. You're going to jail."

"I don't care," I answered, "as long as they will give me water."

In discussion with the soldiers, we learned that rafting this river was, oddly enough, illegal—something we honestly had not known. They quickly realized this and took pity on us, ordering us to go home, clean up, and then file a report at the police station downtown, which we did without further incident.

As we left the station, Carl said, "I still don't have any regrets." Cameron and I agreed, but inside I had to admit I had one regret. When my cousin had made the best suggestion of the trip—that we pray—I had been too ashamed.

Jesus said, "Whoever is ashamed of me and my words, the Son of Man will be ashamed of them when he comes in his glory and in the glory of the Father and of the holy angels" (Luke 9:26).

For the rest of my life, I will tell this story in hopes that it will encourage someone else to jump at the opportunity to pray with others.

Epilogue

The genocide in Rwanda began a year or two after my family had returned to the US. When the UN evacuated the missionaries in Rwanda, Carl stayed. I later learned that during that horrific time, one of the soldiers, who had become a general, saved Carl's life because he recognized him from that day on the bridge.

Camping on Bear Highway

As a child, I imagined myself a rugged mountain man. My favorite books were Kit Carson, Daniel Boone, and Davy Crockett biographies. I spent as much time as I could in the woods trying to get lost so that I could make use of the small survival kit that rode on my belt at all times.

It was my dream to fly into a remote location in Alaska to "survive." On paper, I made lists of what I would take and even designed a raft for the long trip down some forgotten river. In my mind, the only living things I would encounter would be grizzlies, bald eagles, deer, and the like. I would fish, hunt, and live off the land to test myself against nature. The fish would bite anything because they would not know better—having never encountered a human, much less a lure. It was a grand dream, I thought.

My dream finally came true in my late twenties. My college roommate, Greg, and his wife had moved to Alaska, and they invited my wife and me to visit. I knew the trip wasn't going to be quite the way I had imagined as a child, but it was good enough. We wouldn't be floating down a river for a month, living off the land, but we would fly into a semi-remote area to fish. And grizzlies would be our neighbors.

We planned the trip to coincide with the salmon run, and Greg told me that

I could also try "combat fishing," where people stand shoulder to shoulder, thigh-deep in freezing glacier rivers, to catch a few of the millions of salmon returning to spawn. The experience was interesting, but I wouldn't care to do it again.

Finally, we loaded our gear into a six-seat pontoon plane, which floated by the dock. We flew for an hour or so to the Kustatan River, where the pilot landed on a grassy lake, which was more grass than lake. From there, we toted our gear and a small boat motor about half a mile to the river, where a small aluminum boat was kept. Soon we were motoring up the river in search of a good camping and fishing spot. I couldn't see any people besides the four of us, so I was content. I did want to see a bear, though, and they weren't making themselves visible.

We found a good spot to put up our tents, with some woods nearby for firewood. After hurriedly pitching our tents, Greg and I grabbed our rods and waded into the shallow river. Fishing was slow, but I caught a couple of the biggest fish I had ever reeled in. I stashed my stringer of fish back at the bank and was in the middle of the river again when I heard splashing behind me. A teenage grizzly had located my fish. He deliberately lifted the stringer, as though familiar with this method of fishing. He selected the largest fish, and with a tug, he stole it and calmly walked back to the woods to eat his lunch. Signs all over Alaska had already warned me that I could not consider any fish to be my property, and if a bear wanted it, he had the government's permission to take it. I had no right to interfere. So with more watchfulness, I returned to fishing.

The bears remained virtually invisible until after lunch. The four of us relaxed and napped in the warm afternoon. I was preparing to fish some more when I looked back toward the tents, where the others were still napping. There I watched the biggest grizzly in Alaska stroll up to our campsite. He raised himself up to his full forty-five feet (it seemed) to better survey the tents. I yelled, "Bear!" and instantly wondered if it was true that I couldn't outrun a grizzly. I would have considered trying, except I felt I should defend my wife, who was asleep in the tent. But heroic efforts became unnecessary when the bear, obviously impressed by my size, strength, and bravery, decided to leave. My fellow campers scrambled out of their tents in time to see the grizzly amble nonchalantly away.

Evening came, and with it came swarms of bears similar in size to our earlier visitor and similar in number to mosquitoes. Evidently, we had pitched camp smack in the middle of Interstate Grizzly. It was after midnight before things finally quieted down enough to sleep—not that we slept. We kept the fire company all night.

The next day, be it from lack of sleep or dehydration or fear of another sleepless night, I got sick. Sometime in the late morning, oil-well workers bumped along the rough road toward us in a four-wheel drive. We talked to them, and they radioed Anchorage to send our plane that day rather than the next. The fishing was lousy anyway—just two fish, and the biggest one stolen from me. The whole trip was decidedly less than my dreams.

The truth is, we all have dreams, and we work on those dreams, both imagining them and making them come true. Yet more often than not, when we finally get what we dreamed of, it's not what we expected. We "arrive" and end up disappointed. Why? It's because we set our sights too low. We don't dream far enough or big enough. We settle for dreaming shallow dreams.

God has promised a future beyond our wildest dreams—beyond the possibility of imagination. Still, we spend our thoughts and our time working for our earthly dreams. I suppose we deserve the bears that ruin our dreams because we should be dreaming of something so much better.

Consider exchanging your current dreams for "an eternal glory that far outweighs them all" (2 Corinthians 4:17). Start imagining your place in the kingdom of God.

Cultivating Panic

t about eight or nine o'clock one night, my sister disappeared from my parents' house. I was visiting them in Iowa, where they lived on a few acres out in the middle of farmland. The only thing visible from their home was one other house some distance away, so the night was dark and quiet.

My sister was a responsible adult, so her disappearance was no concern at first. We simply wondered where she had gone. Then we called out for her. Not hearing an answer, we called down to the basement. Nothing. We called louder. My dad called outside. Still nothing. Where could she have gone? The vehicles were there, and so were her shoes. Besides, she wouldn't have gone out without mentioning it to us.

My dad can create a supersonic whistle, which he used to call us when we were children. So he tried that a couple of times both inside and outside. No Amy. Panic set in. Thoughts of drive-by kidnappings or accidents in the night began to fill our heads. We prayed without ceasing and understood exactly what that meant as we ran frantically here and there searching.

Finally, we called one of Amy's friends. "Did you come and pick up Amy? We can't find her anywhere." She had not.

For the dozenth time, we searched every room in the house when finally my mother yelled out in relief, "Here she is!" Amy had somehow fallen asleep underneath a pile of blankets at the foot of my parents' bed. During our desperate search, she had slept soundly, oblivious to our calls and unconcerned for her lost condition.

I wonder what the mission of Christ's church would look like right now if we felt for our neighbors even a small fraction of the panic my family felt for my sister that night. This matter of eternal life and eternal death is real, and yet we treat it as though it is the stuff of fairy tales. Could I really have lounged around on the couch that night my sister disappeared and been uninterested in the desperation of my parents? Could I really want to finish my TV program or novel first before helping to locate my lost sister? Of course not.

Angel in a Red Dodge

don't think he was truly an angel. Neither was it a life-and-death situation. I was just driving up the interstate in a very soggy drizzle and had stopped to buy something to drink.

Pulling my Ford pickup in beside a red Dodge truck, I slammed my door and sloshed my way to the covered sidewalk in front of the store. I excused myself past two farmers who stood watching the rain splash at their feet. I bought my drink and pushed the door marked "Pull" as I hurried to get back on the road.

"Lovely day," I smiled facetiously as I again excused myself across their path.

"Actually, it is," said one, breathing in deeply. "We need it."

"Glad it's here then," I said. I ducked into the rain and waded back to my truck. Shoving my key into the ignition, I cranked it. *Click.* I turned it off and tried again. *Click, click, click.*

The man in front of the store watched me as I splashed back toward him. I stood beside him out of the rain considering my options, hoping the downpour would slow.

"Battery shot?" he asked after a while.

"Maybe," I said. "I hope it's only the battery. I'll check the connections and see if something has come loose."

"Need tools? I got some in my truck," he offered.

"No, I have tools. But thanks," I said and prepared to launch back into the rain.

"You got a raincoat too?" asked the farmer.

"Well, no. I guess I don't."

"I do. I'll get it for you." Without waiting for a reply, he ran to his truck and returned with a poncho.

He helped me unravel it, and then I hauled out my toolbox. Grabbing the necessary tools, I popped the hood of my truck, cleaned and tightened my battery cables, then turned the key again. Still nothing. Back in front of the store, the farmer and I discussed what else might be the problem.

"I know where there's a parts store open on Sundays," offered the farmer. "It's about ten miles from here, and they do free battery tests. Let's try to jump-start your truck, and you can follow me there." I offered him his poncho, but he refused. "I live here. You have a long trip to go all wet." Again, without waiting for my reply, he ducked into the rain. We connected the cables, and my truck roared to life.

"I can find the store if you tell me where it is," I said to the farmer as we ran back to shelter. "There's no reason for you to drive all the way there."

"Oh, I don't mind driving there, but actually, it is easy to find." He gave me directions.

I handed back his poncho. "I appreciate your help. Will you let me give you something for your time?" I asked, reaching for my wallet.

He refused. I insisted. "OK, listen," he said. "Someone helped me out a while back. A lot more major than this. He wouldn't let me pay him either. He just asked me to promise I'd help two more people. You're one of them. You promise me the same thing, and we'll call it even."

"It's a deal," I said.

I found the store and purchased a new battery. Heading back toward the interstate, I stopped at a light. A red Dodge pulled up beside me, and the friendly farmer rolled down his window. "I just thought I'd make sure you found the store. Was it just your battery?"

I briefly explained before the light turned green. Then the farmer turned left, and I went straight. I merged onto the interstate, where I began watching the shoulders of the road for anyone who might help me to fulfill my debt to the angel in the red Dodge.

Bait and Switch

was shopping at Best Buy one day when a gentleman approached me. "Do you know much about computers?" he asked. I told him that I knew enough to get around. He said he wanted to buy a printer and wondered if I could give him some advice. Even my limited knowledge was no doubt greater than his, he told me.

As he led me to the printer aisle, he struck up a conversation by asking what my work was. I told him that I worked for my church. "That's great. Faith is important. I thought maybe you worked with computers."

"Well, I work at a computer," I said.

"Do you ever do any work on the side?" he asked.

"As a matter of fact, I do some publication design work sometimes," I replied.

We walked down the printer aisle, and he halfheartedly asked my thoughts about a couple of them, but he seemed more anxious to continue our conversation. "I work for an organization that sometimes needs outside work," he told me. "Could I see what you do?" I was flattered and told him I'd be glad to get my portfolio together and show him. We arranged to meet the next day in the lobby of the Hilton Hotel nearby for an interview.

I arrived before him and set up my laptop computer. When he arrived, we talked for a moment and then I began to show him my work. He didn't pay much attention. Instead, he began to talk about how important family is and how his organization tries to be family-friendly. It was a pleasant conversation, and he assured me that he was interested enough in my work to take me for an interview with his boss and some others.

He gave me the date and location at another hotel and asked that I bring my wife. Since their company was so family-oriented, they would like to meet her too. What a great philosophy for a company, I agreed.

My wife thought it odd that she would have some effect on whether someone gave me design work, but she kindly agreed to accompany me.

The evening arrived, and we found ourselves in a posh hotel conference room. Already a large group had gathered. I was surprised that so many freelancers would be invited to an interview all at the same time.

We took our seats as a slickly dressed man stepped up to the podium. "Good evening, everyone!" he called out enthusiastically. The group responded, "Good evening!" just as enthusiastically. Too enthusiastically. Who *were* these people? Something didn't feel right, but I couldn't put my finger on what. However, things became increasingly clear as the man continued with his questions, and the crowd became increasingly involved. "How many of you value your families? How many of you wish you could stay home with your kids—but your financial situation forces you to work? How many of you want things that you can't afford? You!" He pointed at a lady in the front row. "What do you want that you can't afford?"

"I want a BMW!" she announced loudly.

"Oh yeah!" was the fervent agreement among the group.

I whispered to Becky, "This better not be what I am beginning to think it is." She stifled a giggle and said, "I'm afraid it may be."

The man went on building the crowd to a crescendo of self-indulgence with jargon I couldn't even understand. Finally, he hit us with the punch line. "I'm here to tell you tonight how you can afford to stay home with your kids! I will tell you tonight how you can have your BMW!"

He never actually used the word *Amway* or the phrase "pyramid scheme," but it came across loud and clear. I seethed underneath my dark suit. I had dressed up for this? My Best Buy friend with his family values had duped me!

Through sheer politeness, we waited out the energetic prognosticator of greed. Afterward, my "friend" sidled up to us towing along the man who headed the pyramid scheme. He introduced the man as the president of the organization who asked us what we thought of the presentation. Managing to stay cool and polite, I tried to make it clear that this was not what I had expected and that I wasn't interested. Then the president turned to the man who had invited me and announced woefully, "I'm afraid we don't have a match here." The insult flabbergasted me. Not only did they sucker me there, but now they also didn't even allow me the dignity of turning them down. They rejected *me* as a bad match!

If I were to guess, I would say that authenticity is one of the highest priorities of spiritual seekers today. In reaching out to them, Jesus told us to be both wise as serpents and harmless as doves. Unfortunately, we often tend to operate on the extreme ends of the serpent/dove scale. Serpent-wisdom without dove-harmlessness tempts us toward manipulative techniques. Dove-harmlessness without serpent-wisdom pushes us into irrelevant mediocrity. We need balance.

God's people are not to wear a mask of righteousness. We are to be conscious of and honest about how far we miss the mark of holiness. Neither should we paint idealistic pictures for seekers who will eventually meet a disappointing reality and will feel they have fallen victim to a bait-and-switch scheme. It's good to share the ideal that we all hope one day to reach, but it's also crucial to honestly admit our own inability to live the ideal, to be clear that we are stumbling along together, and that it's only by God's grace that we are moving forward at all.

That's How Rumors Get Started

What tale would your imagination concoct if you heard the following side of a telephone conversation?

"You did what? You killed him! You have him in your trunk? What are you going to do with the body?"

It was around midnight as I drove one of the curving, thickly forested secondary roads of Maryland in my Honda Accord. As my car rounded a curve, my high beams spotlighted the green eyes of a deer in the middle of the road. I slammed on my brakes, and the deer dashed away. I continued driving slowly, peering intently into the glow of my headlights ahead, in case more deer were about.

I should have been watching to the side, too, because suddenly out of the darkness, a deer slammed into me! He crashed into the side of my right front fender, deeply denting it, and then flipped head over tail across my windshield into the opposite lane. I screeched to a stop, and the deer, seemingly unhurt, started to kick his way back onto his feet. Unfortunately, he wasn't fast enough, and a car from the other direction ran over him. That driver must have been fleeing the police or something because he only tapped his brakes before racing away. I was left in the darkness with a dented fender and a dead deer in the middle of the road.

I decided that a good citizen would at least drag the hazard off the road, so I jumped out and dragged the deer to the shoulder of the road. Then I stood and stared at it for a time, pondering what I should do.

I'm a vegetarian, but I still didn't like the idea of leaving a perfectly good deer on the side of the road when it could feed someone for weeks. So, glancing around and seeing no other headlights coming, I opened my trunk and heaved the deer inside.

I inspected my fender to confirm that my car was drivable, and then I drove home. On the way, I wracked my brain, trying to think of someone who might want the deer. It needed to be cleaned and cooled right away. Unfortunately, I could think of no one in suburban Maryland who might take it.

My parents lived close by, so even though it was well after midnight, I called to ask if one of their neighbors might appreciate a freezer full of nice, fresh venison. My dad answered groggily on the second ring. "Hello?" The following words are what my mom, on the other side of the bed, heard that night.

"Jeff! What time is it? Are you all right? You did what?! You killed him? You threw him in your trunk? What are you going to do with the body?"

At this point, I could hear my mother shaking my dad and demanding to know what had happened. My dad and I suddenly realized what my mom was hearing. As I recall, my dad began to exaggerate just for my mom's benefit: "You better just dump the body. Don't let anyone see you! I hope you don't get caught! Don't tell *anyone!*" From the sounds coming over the phone line, my mom was not taking the joke well. Finally, my dad told her that she could relax because what she was imagining was not reality.

You have probably heard and perhaps even said, "Be careful! That's how rumors get started." Had someone else overheard that side of the conversation, I can imagine what could have happened with the story: "Did you hear? Jeff is going to prison for life! He may get the electric chair!"

The wise King Solomon acknowledged how much fun it is to talk about other people—that it's like delicious morsels of food that go down so well (Proverbs 18:8). But talking about others is no joke; it's no feast of conversation. Gossip, says Solomon, separates friends and feeds a quarrel. "Without wood a fire goes out; without a gossip a quarrel dies down" (Proverbs 26:20).

Do you ever sense disunity and a lack of harmony among you and the people around you? Wouldn't you like that kind of negative atmosphere to go away? Why not try jerking the wood out of the quarrel so that it dies for lack of fuel? You can do that if you will stop talking negatively about other people in their absence and be an influence to help others do the same.

Snakes and Cold

Be alert and of sober mind. Your enemy the devil prowls
around like a roaring lion looking for someone to devour.

—1 Peter 5:8

I lived in Minnesota for a number of years. However, I call Tennessee home because that's where my relatives live. Whenever I'm visiting Tennessee, and someone mentions Minnesota, the conversation steers immediately to the weather. "That's where it gets *so* cold!" they say. To warm-weather Southerners, that is all Minnesota is—cold. Very, very cold. The implication is that the weather makes Minnesota unfit for habitation by anything but penguins and polar bears for nine months out of the year; though, everyone admits that the short summers are beautiful.

On the other hand, when I mention Tennessee to Minnesotans, I often find the conversation steers to snakes. "That's where you have poisonous snakes!" they say. The implication is that snakes make Tennessee unfit for habitation because pit vipers lurk under every rock, crawling into your boots during the night, hiding in your bed, intentionally seeking victims to terrorize.

I have lived in Minnesota and have experienced both sides of the equation, and I'm here to tell you that Minnesota winters aren't as bad as Southerners think, nor are poisonous snakes as bad as Minnesotans think.

That said, it is true that when you live in either place, you must make some life adjustments for weather and snakes, respectively. That's why, in Minnesota, I carried a few emergency items in my truck in case I was ever stranded in cold weather. For my wife, a native Minnesotan, carrying these items in her vehicle constituted no adjustment at all. This was normal life for her, and she did it without thinking. Doing so did not make her more concerned about the cold. It was just instinct.

However, she also had to make a small adjustment when we lived in Maryland with poisonous snakes. She had to learn to watch where she stepped. Out of habit, even in Minnesota, I never step over a log or move a large rock or reach my hand into a dark place without checking for snakes. I do it without thinking. Doing so does not make me more concerned about snakes. It's just instinct.

I suppose that until I get stranded in a blizzard, I will be a little cavalier about carrying a payload of cold-weather supplies in my truck. So I can hardly blame Becky for being less careful than I about snakes. I can understand. Thinking about poisonous snakes all the time, rather than relying on instinct to avoid them, actually causes concern. Concern can ruin an otherwise pristine day. So even while living near snakes, Becky didn't think about them all that much—until one day.

We were walking a trail around a small lake. The trail wound through trees and was littered with sticks and forest debris. As always, without thinking, I kept one eye on the trail for any "stick" that might not be a stick at all. That's why I saw a well-camouflaged copperhead just before Becky stepped on it. Not having time to warn her, I stuck out my arm and held her back. I grabbed a stick and poked the snake, which suddenly bounded to life. Becky inhaled loudly and then began to run backward as the snake slithered and even jumped quickly toward her. I'm convinced the snake was heading downhill because that's the direction it was facing, but Becky remains convinced that the serpent chased her.

It's never smart to get so used to snakes or the cold that you forget about the danger they represent. Snakes don't get less poisonous by forgetting them. Minus forty degrees doesn't get less dangerous because you are used to it. Living safely with snakes and the cold requires habitual vigilance. So does living in close proximity to the serpent, called Satan, who would like nothing better than to make your relationship with God grow cold. He is actively looking for victims to terrorize.

The Lady I Avoid

Driving home from work one day, I swung my truck into the entrance to the neighborhood where I lived. I intended to deliver a rent check to the main office that day, but as I rounded the corner, I encountered two minivans parked dead center in the road next to the neighborhood office. Their drivers, presumably mistaking the street for a parlor, were engaged in leisurely conversation. They may have even been sharing tea and scones, though I can't be sure. I swerved in the nick of time, missing both minivans by inches.

As I slowed for the stop sign at the bottom of the hill, I realized that in the excitement, I had forgotten to drop my rent check off at the office. I turned my truck around in the intersection and drove back toward the tea party. The woman in one minivan signaled me to stop, which I did. "You idiot!" she yelled angrily. "Slow down! You nearly hit me just now!"

I responded with the first words that flashed into my mind. "Hey lady, if you didn't treat the road like a parking lot . . ." and so on. Then I turned into the office lot and parked. After delivering my rent check, I saw the lady park her minivan and get out. It was then that I recognized her. She was one of the neighborhood managers. She was a lady who could tell me I had thirty days to pack my bags and leave.

I avoided her from that day forward.

Several weeks later . . .

The group of mailboxes for my street was located on the left side of the road on the far side of the sidewalk. Every day I had to park on the opposite side of the street and get out to retrieve my mail.

I noticed that the sidewalk in front of the mailboxes sloped gently up from one driveway and then back down again at the driveway of the house next door. I reasoned that this was a more efficient way to fetch my mail. All I had to do was drive to the opposite side of the road and run my driver's side wheels up onto the sidewalk. Then I would simply roll down my window to retrieve my mail.

The technique worked well for a couple of weeks until the day the owner of the home behind the mailboxes stormed toward me. I won't repeat what he said, but his words colorfully informed me that I should stop driving on the sidewalk.

A nasty response instantly formed in my mind, but this time I did not succumb to it. Instead, I said, "I'm sorry. I won't do it again."

Those few words were much harder to say than the words I'd bestowed upon my neighborhood manager just weeks before. But these words, so difficult for me to say, stopped my neighbor in his tracks. He was suddenly confused and had to search for different words than he had anticipated using. "Well, OK," he said finally and went back inside. I drove off the sidewalk and home.

Later that same day, I saw the neighbor up the street who had yelled at me, washing his car outside. I walked to his house. "I just wanted to say again that I'm sorry for driving on the sidewalk." I smiled sheepishly. "By the way, I'm Jeff."

He smiled back. "I'm Rob." He shook my hand, and we were friends from that day forward. I didn't have to avoid him.

Jesus said, "Love your enemies, do good to those who hate you, bless those who curse you, pray for those who mistreat you" (Luke 6:27, 28). I see in retrospect how excellent that commandment is.

A Russian Potluck

"So that they may be brought to complete unity.
Then the world will know that you sent me
and have loved them even as you have loved me."
—Jesus, John 17:23

My wife and I lived in Moscow, Russia, for two years. During that time, we began attending the International Adventist Church in downtown, since services were conducted in both English and Russian. It wasn't uncommon to find a dozen or so countries represented at church on a Sabbath morning, including Africans, Central Asians, Arabs, and North and South Americans. (I remember once riding in a van with six people when we were stopped at a police checkpoint. The officer was dumbstruck when the driver of the van gathered and handed him passports from six different countries.) Although the Russians naturally held the majority in our congregation, we had a truly international church—which made for some interesting services.

The African contingent of the congregation was as opposite in personality from the Russians as an Eskimo must be from a desert nomad. One Sabbath morning, the Africans were leading song service, which they do well, even in the challenging Russian language. Everything was fine so long as we sang the hymnal in the minor keys that the Russians so love. But this morning, a young African named Moses announced that we would learn a new song for which we had no Russian translation. We would all do it in English—not that this was so unusual for this church. What was unusual was the upbeat tempo and that we all had to hold hands, swing our arms, and sing, "Welcome! Welcome! How do you do? Happy to see you! Happy to meet you! Welcome! Welcome! How do you do?"

To fully appreciate the effect this had on the Russians, you really must walk the streets of Moscow—or even attend church—to feel the depth of somberness that often permeates the society in public places. You simply don't act like the Africans were suggesting—especially not in church. Such obvious joy was considered frivolous.

As I observed the giant flop the Africans had introduced, I thought to myself, *They won't do that again!* I was wrong. The next week they sang the song again with reluctant participation. The third week, however, I noticed a slight change in the congregation. They were warming up to the song. By week number four, "Welcome! Welcome! How do you do?" had become a firmly entrenched favorite. They probably still sing it. Even the stone-faced babushkas (grandmothers) were snatching the hands of fellow worshipers and flinging them high over their heads, singing with smiles on their faces. I was impressed with their acceptance and the unity that it inspired in our church. This was not the kind of attitude you found in Moscow generally speaking, but here, among God's people, unity (and joy along with it) broke through.

Even as I commended the Russians in the congregation for their flexible spirits, I was privately waging my own tiny war against them, just as I suspected they had done to the Africans. For me, the issue centered around potluck.

Potluck, I discovered, is not a Russian tradition. It seems that in Russia, the concept of everyone bringing food to put together is limited, perhaps, to a family picnic. Not that they were against the idea, but they simply had not heard of it before. So we introduced it.

The first week, potluck began well. Everyone brought their food and placed it on a long table. Just as we were getting ready to eat, a babushka grabbed the stack of plates and plasticware that had been neatly placed at the head of the table and lined them up, side by side, down both sides of the long table.

Not wanting to embarrass her, we adjusted the instructions. Rather than lining up to get a plate, we would now grab the nearest plate and then rotate around the table to get our food. Everyone nodded approvingly, and we said grace. At "Amen!" everyone dug happily into whatever dishes were nearest them and chowed down. No one rotated. They simply stood there eating and talking together, having a grand time. Our calls over the noise to "Rotate!" went unheeded. We were stuck eating the food in front of us, like it or not. It just wasn't right! It wasn't potluck the way it was supposed to be.

The next week, we were extra clear on the instructions to line up. When the babushkas began to distribute the plates, we gathered them back up and herded everyone into a line. The line did move—but only because those who had not yet gotten to the table kept urging the "snackers" forward. Eventually, everyone had a spot at the table and once again stood over their small domain of food, eating happily, deaf to all encouragement to rotate around or find a seat.

The next week, the plates were again distributed around the table, and I dished myself up a serving of discontentment at how uncooperative everyone was. That is until I finally noted that I seemed to be the only discontented one in the bunch.

Who made the rule that potluck has to be conducted the way I remember it, anyway? No one, of course. And with that liberating thought, suddenly my own horizons broadened, and I could enjoy my fellow Christians again in unity brought about by flexibility and acceptance—not someone else's but my own.

Jesus called His people to unity, not uniformity. Uniformity is acting and thinking alike. Unity is enjoying being together even though we don't act or think alike.

Andrei's Story

Temperatures regularly soar above one hundred during the summer in Central Asia. Arid desert hills dotted with tufts of dry grass and the occasional brightly robed shepherd and his goats are sometimes the only movement outside of the cities. Even inside the cities, air conditioning is a luxury afforded only by the rich, so the common people make the most of the huge sycamore trees lining their streets. The heat slows life to a more comfortable crawl—except at one house in a city located about an hour and a half's drive south of the capital of this country.

That was the home of Andrei and Ludmila, who, at the time, looked to be in their late thirties or early forties. Andrei's wife, Ludmila, of Korean descent, is slim and silent with a mouthful of gold teeth. Andrei, of Russian descent, is short and built like a tree trunk. His face is a contrast of hardened features and a smile. His eyes are kind, but you feel they've not always been.

Face to face with Andrei, you feel an energy out of place in the slow-moving life surrounding his neighborhood. The living room of their home lacks the standard couch/bed, table, and chairs common to homes in that area.

Andrei has not always been a Christian, much less a Seventh-day Adventist Global Mission pioneer. In fact, the story of his journey to Christ began in prison, where he was on death row. Andrei was twenty-three years old. He had gotten involved in a life that led him deeper and deeper into the world of organized crime. He had been involved in a shooting—the wrong place at the wrong time is how he described it.

For six months, Andrei sat awaiting execution and thinking about his life. "The realization that you are so young, and they are going to kill you is brutally sobering," admits Andrei. "I was depressed and lonely. I couldn't eat. It was then that I began to feel an unknown presence around me, which comforted me. It felt like the warmth of a father that I had never had," he said.

For unexplained reasons, Andrei's death sentence was commuted to fifteen years in prison with hard labor in the uranium mines. But that was nothing more than trading one death sentence for another. Men sent to the mines soon lost their hair and then their teeth, growing weaker and weaker from radiation poisoning until they finally died. Andrei worried about his own fate, but after some time, he realized that nothing was happening to him. For six years, Andrei worked in the uranium mines with no side effects whatsoever.

Then an epidemic of typhoid swept through the prison. Andrei said that at one point, he carried ten bodies out of the prison in a single day. Eventually, Andrei contracted the disease himself, and after five days, he knew he lay close to death. He couldn't turn over or even open his eyes.

Then about 3:00 A.M. one morning, Andrei awoke as someone turned him from his left side to his right, and suddenly he could open his eyes. Before him stood two identical young men in shining clothes. "I don't remember what they looked like," says Andrei, "but I remember their eyes. Such pleasant faces. They looked into my eyes and leaned over me. They didn't speak. I felt as though I knew them, and that I had known them all of my life. Finally, they left, but I saw that they did not walk. I thought God was telling me I was dying, and I realized that I was not ready to meet the Lord." But from that moment, without medicine, Andrei began to get well.

When perestroika came to the Soviet Union, the uranium mines were closed for a time, and the prisoners had nothing to do. So the prison officials invited Orthodox, Buddhist, and Krishna missionaries to the prison for entertainment. But Andrei explained that the pressures of criminal life are as strong inside prison as outside, and his high position in the world of crime did not allow him to talk to religious people. But when they handed out Bibles, Andrei secretly approached one of the men and asked for one.

He didn't have any grand ideas about the Bible, but he was curious about how old the world was and hoped that maybe the Bible could tell him. He discovered the genealogies and started calculating. Sometimes he got mixed up and had to back up to the beginning and count again. It was during his search for the age of the earth that Andrei began to accept the Lord he was encountering in the Bible.

As his conviction grew, he felt he should pray. But at first, he could not bring himself to drop to his knees before anyone. His pride was too great for such humility. Finally, though, his feelings became so intense that he fell to his knees and prayed.

Andrei's criminal life still haunted him. The leaders of the crime world had big plans for him. They had been preparing him to become the leader of several prisons. Finally, Andrei approached them and told them that he felt he could not continue his life in this way. He felt that God was calling him. He left the criminal groups he normally associated with. The leaders became concerned and began to interrogate him. They sent people to make his life miserable. But he tried to respond in the way he was learning from the Bible.

Later, Andrei was transferred to another prison in the mountains. Most of the prisoners there were local indigenous people, and Andrei didn't speak their language, only Russian. Andrei knew he would never be allowed to communicate with anyone on the outside about his new beliefs, so he organized a group of fifteen men in prison who also spoke Russian and were willing to study the Bible together.

One day, they were meeting outside in the prison compound when the guards became suspicious and began to question them in the local language. To his own surprise, Andrei began to answer them in their language. The members of his group were shocked. The guards left and didn't bother them again.

Andrei's group didn't know how to conduct a worship service, but he says that the Holy Spirit gave them ideas. They would study a particular book of the Bible. One person would study ahead and then present his findings to the group. Later, Andrei was very pleased to discover this was essentially Sabbath School.

One day their group study came to a halt—at the fourth commandment. The group was astounded and curious. How could Saturday be the seventh day? The Orthodox calendar, which all Orthodox countries use, sets Sunday as the seventh day. The group could not solve the problem, so they finally skipped over it and went on. Two months later, the problem presented itself to Andrei's mind again. He asked himself if he should believe God's calendar or man's.

As a group, they decided that Saturday was the holy day. So now they had to keep it, which was not an easy choice. Three of the fifteen resolved to keep the Sabbath.

At first, Andrei traded work shifts with other prisoners so that he would not have to work on Sabbath. But after six months, his conscience wouldn't allow him to ask others to break the Sabbath. About that time, Andrei was sent to "adaptation," which prepares prisoners for life in the outside world again by having them work outside the prison and sleep inside.

One of the prison officials put Andrei in charge of the electricity for all the buildings and equipment—a job with significant responsibility. Andrei fervently prayed that nothing would ever break down on Sabbath. Up until that time, God had been helping him to find ways to keep the Sabbath. However, the prison officials soon learned that he was trying to keep the Sabbath, and they began to give him trouble. "Fix this car right now," they would say. "It's nothing. It will just take two minutes. At least just look at it." Andrei begged them to let him wait until after Sabbath.

That is when Andrei says his troubles really began. They locked him into a horrible cell, but Andrei felt God's presence there, and he knelt and asked Christ to forgive them.

It all came to a head one day when the prison officials surrounded him and demanded to know why he refused to work on Saturdays. Andrei explained his commitment to God and that he couldn't break it—not even in a small matter. He even appealed to them to join him in honoring God.

Then, Andrei says, it seemed that Satan began speaking directly through his boss. He jumped onto a table, his eyes glowing with anger. "I have never done anything wrong before God!" he shouted. Andrei, terrified, broke out in a cold sweat.

"Make your choice!" the man screamed. "If you don't start working when you're told, you will be sorry." Andrei understood they intended to beat him, even to death, as often happened.

Andrei prayed urgently as the men picked up various weapons and surrounded him. "Choose. If you keep Sabbath, we will break you."

Andrei asked for some water to clean himself up. They gave it to him. He washed, and then he said, "OK, I'm ready to give up my life." For ten minutes they kept themselves busy with their weapons, but no one began the attack.

Finally, one officer shouted, "Go! But when Sabbath comes, stay in your cell and don't walk around letting people see you not working." Andrei agreed.

Then they called together the prisoners and ordered them not to listen to anything Andrei might say to them. Then they ordered him never to preach, but Andrei could not agree to this demand.

Not long afterward, the man who had jumped on the table and shouted at Andrei had a heart attack and spent two months in the hospital. When he returned, he informed Andrei that their country's constitution allowed him to keep his beliefs. "But I have my own law," he told Andrei. "If I see you ever sit down for even five minutes during your work, I'll send you straight back to the mines."

He gave Andrei five jobs. All day, every day, he worked. He used the nights to study his Bible. He received only one meal each night until he finally collapsed. He was sent to a clinic, where the doctor informed him that water was collecting in his lungs. He remained in the hospital for a year, and despite being in bed with a burning fever, Andrei found opportunities to preach to the people around him.

When Andrei didn't recover, he was finally set free because of his poor health, and the rest of his sentence was commuted. He immediately drove to the capital and found a Sabbath-keeping church—the Seventh-day Adventist Church—where he was soon baptized.

Andrei's health returned, and eventually he was invited to serve as a Global Mission pioneer in the same city where he spent so many years in prison. Right away, Andrei went and preached in the very spot where prison officials had ordered him never to preach again. Then he handed out an entire box of books to the men there.

I remember when I was with a large group of pioneers in that country discussing their work. Andrei was there also. One after the other, they complained about the difficulties in their cities, how no one would listen, how the authorities made it impossible to work by ordering them to stop. They were ready to quit, to give up. Andrei sat quietly and shook his head sadly as he listened.

Knowing his story, I easily guessed the reason. After what he had been through, he was fearless in his work for the Lord.

"Who shall separate us from the love of Christ? Shall trouble or hardship or persecution or famine or nakedness or danger or sword? As it is written: 'For your sake we face death all day long; we are considered as sheep to be slaughtered.' No, in all these things we are more than conquerors through him who loved us. For I am convinced that neither death nor life, neither angels nor demons, neither the present nor the future, nor any powers, neither height nor depth, nor anything else in all creation, will be able to separate us from the love of God that is in Christ Jesus our Lord" (Romans 8:35–39).

Siberian Adventure

I t was the middle of December when I flew with Valery Ivanov from Moscow to Irkutsk. When we landed, it was about 4:00 A.M. and -25 degrees Fahrenheit.

From Irkutsk, we rode the Trans-Siberian Railway to the city of Chita. In Chita, a local pastor had arranged for a van and two drivers to transport us the final four hundred miles over the barren, frozen Siberian roads to the shared borders of Russia, China, and Mongolia, where we were to meet two church planters working in the city of Krasnokamensk.

Before leaving Chita, we stopped for gas. The driver filled the van and also two jerry cans in the back. I assumed we would see no gas stations after this, but my assumption was not correct. We could find gas stations, but we couldn't trust the gas/water mixtures to actually run the van.

I sat bundled in my down parka in the back of the van, silently begging the heat to reach me. I soon realized, however, that the heater worked only in the front. This didn't turn out to be the problem I expected, though, because numbness mercifully gained control of my toes, and they didn't really feel cold. In fact, they didn't feel anything.

Through the window, I watched the frozen, windswept hills of Siberia crawl by, passing village after village of brightly painted houses, which, despite the paint, presented the general color of black, due to coal dust and frozen mud.

After stopping for dinner at a dubious-looking restaurant, we climbed back into the van. The driver turned the ignition, but the van refused to start. A half hour of experimentation finally rewarded us with the knowledge that holding a wrench on the battery in just the right position allowed the van to start. We chugged along for about fifteen minutes until the van began to sputter. It was out of gas. The jerry cans of gasoline quickly filled the tank, and we were off again.

Another fifteen minutes or so and again the van sputtered, coughed, and lurched to a stop. We were not out of gas. I know a little about engines, but what happened over the next hour or so really baffled me. It involved disassembling the carburetor and attaching a tire pump to pump out the "better" gas we got in Chita.

The Russians, and Siberians in particular, are incredibly resourceful people, and after a while, the drivers had the van running again—for a few minutes. The same scenario repeated itself two or three more times until finally it got dark and the temperature plummeted.

I still couldn't feel my feet, and I was losing feeling in my legs. After another carburetor-pumping scenario, we left the last sizable town we would see before our destination. Before us was nothing but Siberia smothered in blackness and subzero temperatures. I watched the few lights of town fade behind us with a strange sense of foreboding. Finally, the last light disappeared, and only the stars lit the night, and again the van came to a halt. This time we ground and popped to the side of the road—we were dealing with something much more serious than a sticky carburetor this time. A quick look under the van by the light of a flaming gas torch, and the driver announced that we had lost some bolts in the transmission, which was now separating from the engine. We weren't going anywhere.

Jack London stories filled my mind. I wanted to be home in my own warm, soft bed. We waited. We could do nothing else. Finally, a pair of headlights broke the horizon, and a semi-truck roared toward us. Our driver flagged him, and he stopped. The truck driver listened to our plight and then rummaged around in his cab until he came up with a bolt of some sort, which miraculously, as far as I'm concerned, they used to reattach the transmission to the engine.

I breathed a sigh of relief when I learned that we would not proceed deeper into the Siberian freezer that night. The van slowly limped back to town, where we hoped to find a hotel for the night. We did, and I slept well.

"Today, we hire a Russian Cadillac," my translator proudly informed me the next morning. It was a Toyota. It might as well have been a Cadillac, for it bore us speedily and warmly to the border town of Krasnokamensk.

Krasnokamensk had once been just a small village, but Soviet geologists had discovered uranium there, and plans were made to turn the village into a metropolis. They had barely begun when communism fell and all work stopped, half completed. Radiation levels, I am told, are eight times higher than normal.

It was there that I met Ivan and Yevgeni. They had arrived in Krasnokamensk a couple of months earlier to plant a church.

At their small apartment, they served us a large lunch of soup, bread, and other good Russian food. After lunch, they took us to the town center, a warehouse of sorts, where they proudly showed us the corner where they had been given permission to set up shop. There, on a makeshift board, they displayed a variety of spiritual books. My translator explained to me why these young church planters were able to have such a display. They had been given three months of a stipend (about thirty-five dollars a month) all at once. This is what they were to live on for three months. Instead of using it for living expenses, however, they spent the entire amount on books. The only way they were able to eat and pay rent was if people bought their books. I was suddenly glad I hadn't eaten much.

Fortunately, Ivan was a basketmaker and could use that skill to help them survive. For instance, he had come to Siberia without a coat that could withstand the harsh winter, so he made a basket for which someone traded him a good coat. His slippers were tied together with twine.

I asked them what the most challenging part of their work was. I was dumbstruck when Ivan told me that he missed his wife and newborn daughter, whom he had left behind in Ukraine to move to Krasnokamensk to plant this new church. What a sacrifice he was making.

Both Ivan and Yevgeni could have told me story after story of their struggles, but mostly they talked enthusiastically about their work. In two months, they already had a group of twenty people meeting together, and several were almost ready for baptism. What impressed me most was their one-track minds. Everything they did had one purpose. I doubt a minute slipped by when they weren't thinking, *How can I introduce Jesus to this person or that person?*

Seeing and talking with them, I had to ask myself, *What sacrifices do I make to bring Jesus to someone else? Cold toes for a week in Siberia? Ridiculous!* After I left Krasnokamensk, winter really hit, and heat was a luxury not to be had at any price. Entire buildings were cloaked in thick ice.

Thank God for those who, without counting the cost, never let a moment slip by without thinking, *What can I do right now to introduce Jesus to the people around me?*

Scammed

While I was living in Russia, my boss from the US, Mike, flew over to tour some projects in Central Asia. He and I were going to travel from there through Kyrgyzstan and Uzbekistan to Tajikistan. I had already flown from Moscow to Almaty, the largest city in Kazakhstan. Mike was to arrive around 11:00 P.M. that night. Since someone else was going to meet him at the airport, I went to bed to get over my jet lag.

When I awoke the next morning, I found out that Mike had gone missing. When someone from our office went to pick him up at the airport the night before, they found that the last flight had arrived early, and the airport had already closed. It wasn't a large airport, and the officer on duty assured them that Mike had indeed arrived and had taken a taxi.

If Mike is anything, he's a seasoned traveler. He spends much of his time in the airports of many different countries. And though crime is common in Almaty, it would take a pretty brave criminal to take advantage of someone Mike's size. So no one worried that night. Mike had probably just found a hotel and would call in the morning. However, when he didn't call the next morning, we began to be concerned.

We gave two secretaries the task of calling every hotel in the city, while the rest of us went to morning worship. After worship, I discovered they still had not located Mike. There were only two more hotels to call. Finally, the Sheraton, the last hotel on the list, said, "Yes, Mike is here."

We cheered, and they transferred us to his room. Mike answered, "Oh, hello, I was wondering when you were going to call."

"What do you mean?" we asked. "After we didn't find you at the airport, we didn't know where you might be. We've called every hotel in town, hoping you might be at one of them and not dead in a gutter somewhere."

Well, to make a long story short, Mike had been scammed, and the airport staff was in on it. They got his name—probably from an airport worker or from his luggage—and approached him. "Are you Mike? Welcome to Kazakhstan! I have your car outside." Mike had expected to have to wait for his ride since the plane was early, so he was pleasantly surprised. Meanwhile, the person who had actually been sent to meet him was redirected by the officer outside. When Mike finally exited the airport, he noted that it was a hired car that awaited him, but that wasn't suspicious. The man loaded his luggage and drove him into town to the Sheraton—about a fifteen-minute ride.

"They want me to stay here tonight?" Mike asked since he had expected to stay in one of the guest rooms at the church office.

"Yes, they will call you in the morning. That will be two hundred dollars, please." Mike had started to open his door and stopped.

"How much? Did you say two hundred dollars for a fifteen-minute ride?"

"Yes, sir."

"I won't pay you that much," said Mike, understanding that he was being ripped off. He generously gave the man fifty dollars and said, "If you don't like that, then take me back to the airport." The man decided to take it.

So all's well that ends well. Mike avoided the money part of the scam, thanks to his experience, but he didn't avoid the first part. And how could he have? There was no reason even to be suspicious.

Jesus said in Mark 13:22, "For false messiahs and false prophets will appear and perform signs and miracles to deceive, if possible, even the elect." Have you ever considered how the final great deception that Satan is engineering for planet Earth could fool so many people—so many Christians? From my study, it appears to me that the great lie is going to look like God's honest truth to everyone except those intimately acquainted with the Word of God.

The only way Mike could have avoided the scam was if he had been forewarned of this particular trick. Fortunately, the Bible does exactly that for God's "elect." It forewarns us of a coming deception when Satan will masquerade as Christ Himself and lead the world after him. We can recognize the scam if we take the time now to become intimately acquainted with Jesus and His Word.

Standing on the Promises
While Stomping on the Priorities

Once upon a time, I was entirely content when I ordered, say, a software package and could receive it by mail within a week. Then overnight service became available, and suddenly two days was a long wait. Now if it takes longer than two minutes to download my software from the internet, I tap my desk impatiently.

My wife, Becky, has always been intrigued by the simplicity of the Amish lifestyle. So on our second anniversary, I took her to Lancaster County, Pennsylvania, a couple of hours away from our home at the time. We traveled the countryside, sampled the local restaurants, and toured a model Amish farm and the visitor center. As we came to understand more of the Amish way of life, we wondered at the seeming arbitrariness of their theology and lifestyle. An Amish boy can own a scooter but not a bicycle. A family can install a telephone in the barn but not in the house. They can use DC power but not AC. Initially, it all seemed hypocritical and pharisaical to me. I might still think so if Becky wasn't the voracious reader that she is.

As we drove, she read to me how one of the Amish elders explained their rules. He honestly admitted that the lines they have drawn are indeed arbitrary. But what makes the difference in Amish society is the simple fact that they have lines. These lines, said the elder, were not always lines of morality but rather threads that hold their fabric of life together. This fabric is their families.

A scooter allows a boy to travel a little faster, but it keeps him closer to home than a bicycle would. A telephone in a barn covers emergencies and necessities, but it doesn't interrupt family dinner or wake family members up at night. Battery power rules out television, but it keeps the milk cold.

In a word, the arbitrary lines of the Amish safeguard their *time*—time to spend with God and family—the priorities that they set, not that society sets for them.

I am afraid that I am but vaguely aware of my own shortcomings in drawing lines to protect these two most important priorities in life. And as a pastor it's too easy to rationalize that my work, a service to God Himself, ought to take priority over my personal relationship with Him and the people He has given me to care for. Oswald Chambers, in his sermons compiled in the book *My Utmost for His Highest,* says, "The greatest competitor of true devotion to Jesus is the service we do for Him."[1]

How often have you skipped morning devotions because you stayed up too late the night before? And how often can blame for that late night be placed on work or television, as opposed to talking to your husband or wife, playing with your kids, or prayer?

Why do we allow our priorities to get out of line? For most humans, the temptation is ambition—the ruthless quest for money and power. However, for many religious people, Christians included, ambition can take on a more frightening form—a supposed devotion to God.

Evil doesn't care why I fail to uphold important priorities, as long as I fail.

A colleague once gave me a pointed one-sentence sermon in the form of a question. He asked, "Are you busier than Jesus was?" Ouch.

Let's reevaluate our priorities and put our relationship with Jesus Christ first each day.

1. Oswald Chambers, *My Utmost for His Highest* (Grand Rapids: Discovery House Publishers, 2019), January 18; https://utmost.org/it-is-the-lord/.

Hugging a Dirty Boy

At about a year and a half old, my son ate like a tornado. He hurled large chunks of milk-soaked bread, tomato-laden macaroni, or demolished banana in all directions and all over himself.

As a star-struck dad, I was perhaps more effective in teaching him such things as how to hug than I was in teaching him table manners. Therefore, he quickly learned how to swing his arms wide and call out, "HUG!" Naturally, in this case, he always got what he asked for. I dropped everything and smothered him in hugs—until one day.

I was on dinner duty. True to form, my son had plastered himself from head to toe with globs of food. Suddenly, a devious spark sprang into his eyes, and I saw trouble brewing. Loading his hands with food, he flung his arms wide, grinned at me, and called out, "HUG!"

I hesitated, looking at his beaming, messy face, and then I reached for a dishrag. I faked a huge grin and said, "I know, let's clean you up first!" He shook his head vigorously. "HUG!" he demanded.

Suddenly, a thought leaped into my mind (maybe that was because I'm a pastor and I'm always looking for sermon illustrations). For whatever reason, though, at that moment I thought how Jesus must see me. I've made such a mess out of my life, as we all have. We plaster ourselves inside and out with the ugliest, messiest sins we can think of. We fill our minds and bodies with every kind of perversion we can invent. We spread our evil to everyone and every place around us. We are not a pretty sight.

Unlike my son, however, we usually feel so guilty about our mess that we don't dare come to Jesus. Sure, we have heard that He loves us so much that He was willing to die for us. But still we feel that we are too messed up to call out to Him. We are convinced that we must clean ourselves up before we have the right to accept the love of Jesus.

Jesus has no such thoughts about you. He doesn't hesitate and look for a dishrag first, as I did with my son. If you call out to Jesus to come into your life, He will do it in a flash. You will notice that Jesus did not say, "Come to Me all you who have it together and have cleaned yourselves up, and then will I give you rest." He said exactly the opposite, "Come to me, all you who are weary and burdened, and I will give you rest" (Matthew 11:28).

All of this ran quickly through my mind as I stared at my messy little boy with his arms flung wide looking expectantly up to me. Out of principle, I dropped the dishrag and wrapped my clean arms around him. I came away with food on my shirt, my arms, my face—and he came away a little bit cleaner than he had been before the hug.

Isaiah says that Jesus took up our infirmities and our sorrows (Isaiah 53:4). He was pierced and crushed for our sins, and He took our punishment (verses 5, 6). In effect, He hugs us with all our dirtiness. And every time we call to Him, He comes into our lives, and He takes our mess upon Himself and leaves us clean.

Incredible! Absolutely incredible! Don't fool yourself into thinking you can clean yourself up enough to deserve your hugs from Jesus. The only way you can become clean is through His hug. Don't wait. Throw your arms open wide, call for Him, and He will overwhelm you with His love. Do it today. Do it now.

HUG YOU!

As I worked outside one day, my son played nearby. He suddenly spied the open doors to the shed where I store the riding lawn mower, among many sharp gardening implements. The green John Deere lawn mower ranked at the top of his list of favorite toys because it matched his little green John Deere tractor in the house. However, he knew that he was not allowed to go into the shed unaccompanied by Daddy.

I watched the wheels turn in his mind as he stared at the beckoning doors. He quickly lost the battle to temptation, and I saw the decision switch from whether or not to proceed to whether or not he could outrun me. Since I appeared to be ignoring him, he decided to try. First, he edged farther away, as though he was simply playing in a different spot. Then he began to walk nonchalantly away from me. I called to him, "Stay here with me, please."

He stopped, looked at me, then at the shed again. He pointed and said, "Tractor?"

"Yes, that's a tractor, but you need to stay here with me." He edged farther away. When I put down my pruners, he bolted. I called, "Stop!" He didn't. He wasn't in any danger yet, but the fact that he had deliberately disobeyed me made my temperature rise, and I ran after him.

Before he reached the door of the shed, I grabbed him from behind and picked him up. "I told you to stop," I said firmly. "You must listen to me when I call you."

He struggled to get away, so I turned his little face toward mine and looked him in the eye. "Do you understand that you must obey me?" I asked sternly. He stared at me for a second and then burst into a loud wail! However, this was not a tantrum because of not being allowed to do what he wanted—but rather a wail of despair, a wail of deeply hurt feelings. He recognized that I was upset with him, and it seemed to break his little heart.

What he did next brought tears to my own eyes. Rather than struggling violently to get away, rather than fearing the wrath of his father, he flung himself upon my mercy and screamed, "HUG YOU! HUG YOU!" (He meant "hug me," but he didn't have the "me" concept figured out yet.)

In a flash, all the "wrath" that had risen in me disappeared, and I enveloped my son in a bear hug. I immediately pondered what he had just taught me.

The reason I wanted my son to obey me is because I didn't want him to get hurt. I wanted him to develop a habit of obedience because someday it might really mean the difference between life and death for him. I wasn't angry with my son the way some might think of anger. What I felt may be something like the wrath that God feels toward me sometimes—a wrath of love. When I feared that my son was not learning to obey me, I responded with controlled "wrath" so that he would get the point. I deeply wanted him to understand that Dad is serious when he calls, "Stop!" The consequences of him not learning this were too terrifying to think about for long.

Jesus said, "Those whom I love I rebuke and discipline" (Revelation 3:19). Sometimes God "shouts" at us by not protecting us from the consequences of our actions. Time and again, I have found myself stuck in a predicament, humiliated in front of people, at a loss for a way out of a situation, and I recognize, sometimes later rather than sooner, that God is trying to speak to me through the situation. He is calling to me, "Stop! Listen to Me!"

When I look Him in the eyes and I see how deeply He loves me and why He wants me so badly to obey Him, I have two choices: I can fight and struggle to get away so that I can go my own way, or I can call out to Him at the top of my lungs, "HUG YOU!"

If I choose the second option, He'll wrap me in His bear hug and weep with joy because I just learned a valuable lesson that someday could mean the difference between eternal life or death for me. And that is what matters most to Him—that I choose life with Him.

Shamu: My Hero

One year, my family and I left the cold and snow of Minnesota for a week's vacation in Florida with my parents. We went to soak up the sun, but SeaWorld sounded interesting. We had heard of trained whales, dolphins, birds, and so on, and finally we decided to visit. We weren't disappointed. There were enough animals having fun with humans to keep our boys in wonder for hours.

The biggest attraction at SeaWorld was Shamu the orca whale. But there was only one show per day, so we planned for it. We visited the other animals that were in close proximity to Shamu's theater until about an hour before the program. It was then that we noticed a surge in the number of people going in one direction.

"Maybe we should go now to be sure we get a seat," I suggested. So we merged with the masses heading for Shamu. When we arrived, the line before the unopened doors was already stretching out. Obviously, this was going to be a great show.

Becky and I took the boys to see another exhibit nearby while my parents held a place in line. When they had found seats, my dad called me on my cell phone to tell me where they were. We rushed to the stadium and scanned the large crowd until we spotted my dad waving from midway up the stands.

Finally, seated and ready, all went quiet and on the huge screen appeared a moving tribute to servicemen and women. Tears jerked from people's eyes as they honored America's heroes.

Then the music started, and the show began. As the crowd cheered, the performers swam, dived, and skied; the whales leapt out of the water, did tricks, and splashed the crowd. My boys were thunderstruck. I never once had to tell them to pay attention or be still. And it never occurred to me that I needed to.

Suddenly, the music changed. Drums began pounding, and the whale trainers each ran to a section of the bleachers and started stirring up the crowd. Quickly, everyone began to follow their lead in time with the drums. Clap, clap, raise hands, shout, "Shamu!" Clap, clap, raise hands, shout, "Shamu!"

Oddly, it reminded me of the temple scene from *Indiana Jones and the Temple of Doom*. Startled by the thought, I tore my eyes away from the action and looked at the crowd. That's when it dawned on me what we were doing. We were worshiping! True, we were worshiping performers, whales, and soldiers, but all the elements of true worship were there, including the hearts and souls of the people.

We are made to worship, and if we don't fill that inner drive by worshiping God, we will find other ways to fill it. I suppose that is why celebrities are followed with such godlike devotion.

I admit, I enjoyed the worship experience the creators of Shamu provided. I admit that I enjoyed it more than many worship services focusing on God. You see, I don't remember the last time I joined a large crowd moving toward church, anxious to find a seat before they were all taken. I must think hard to remember the last time the worship service was choreographed, practiced, and executed beautifully. I don't remember the last time someone put together a moving tribute to God, or even to frontline missionaries, that jerked tears from the crowd. I don't remember the last time that delighted and happy people shouted out praises to God at the top of their lungs.

No, we save all of that for SeaWorld—and someday, for heaven. But the truth is, we don't have to wait. "I rejoiced with those who said to me, 'Let us go to the house of the LORD' " (Psalm 122:1).

Celebrating "Me" Events

I t's a new day in a home when children learn to read because then they can broach subjects that parents know nothing about. At one point, my son was infatuated with the calendar and its list of holidays and celebrations inside the United States and outside, as well as inside Christianity and outside.

A while back, he asked what Rosh Hashanah was. With a little help from an encyclopedia, I explained that it was the Jewish New Year. "What food do they eat and can we eat that?" he wanted to know. So we did.

Then he wanted to know what Passover was. I explained that is when the Jews remember the Exodus out of Egypt. "What did they eat?" I didn't need the encyclopedia for that one. Unleavened bread and bitter herbs. "Can we eat that?" he asked. So we did.

Then he wanted to know about Sukkot. I definitely needed the encyclopedia for that one. "Ah, that's the Feast of Booths. That's when the Jews remembered living in the wilderness for forty years."

"What did they eat?" I was beginning to see a distinct agenda to his study of the calendar.

Then he began to ask about Muslim holidays, which I was entirely clueless about. That is until he got to Ramadan. That one I knew from my time in the Middle East. "Daddy, what is *Raaaa-maaaa-daaaa-n?*" I instantly saw the promise in what was about to transpire.

"It's a Muslim holiday that lasts a whole month!" I replied enthusiastically. He also instantly saw the promise in what he thought was about to transpire.

"What do they eat?"

I looked him dead in the eye, "They don't."

His eyes looked confused and then widened. "For a whole month?"

"Just during the day," I said. "They eat at night. It's called fasting." I watched the mental wheels spin to the point of overheating.

"Daddy?"

"Yes."

"I don't want to celebrate Ramadan."

"No? Not at all?"

Nope!

"How about for just one week?"

He shook his head.

"Maybe a couple of days?"

Still no.

"Just one day?"

"I know," he said. "I'll celebrate Ramadan for part of one meal." Then he qualified further, "A meal that doesn't have treats." Spoken like a human being.

Holidays in general, and religious celebrations in particular, are intended to draw our thoughts to something great, to give us an opportunity to reflect on the meaning of some historical high point or grand theme. The hope is that in such remembrance we will live differently today. We will be more grateful, more willing to give of ourselves, more likely to live in unity with others, and so on.

But we have made holidays in large part about the food, or the presents. Why? Because, ultimately, we like to feel good, and good food makes us feel good, and getting stuff makes us feel good. We have managed to turn holidays into "me" events.

We've done the same with church. We are prone to selfishness even in matters of religion. Perhaps now would be a good time to think about the purpose of church, which is a celebration in its own rite. Perhaps it's time to think of what we can bring to it more than what it can bring to us.

The Look-At-Me Effect

I remember an experience I had after I bought a new truck. Well—a used truck—but new to me. I had been looking for quite a while, so when I found one that I could afford, I pounced on it. The problem was that it was jacked up, had a loud performance exhaust system, and sported fancy, oversized wheels. My boys loved it, but I told them not to get attached to these accessories because I was going to transform it from a teenager truck into a regular truck again. They demanded an explanation for such irrational behavior. I tried to explain but couldn't seem to put my underlying thoughts into appropriate words. Hoping that an example might help, I told them that the first comment I had heard from someone was, "Fancy wheels, Pastor!" To me, this seemed like a problem, but my boys viewed this in a positive light.

I took the truck to town and asked the muffler guy what it would take to quiet my "performance exhaust system." When he raised it up on the lift, he laughed out loud and said, "This is a performance exhaust system? The muffler has just been removed." It was an easy fix.

Next, I researched how to tackle the lift kit and the wheels, but I was informed that changing this could be pretty expensive. So I had a conversation with myself. Was it right to spend unnecessary money just to satisfy whatever it was that was bothering me about this truck? At first, I decided no. Better to leave it alone. My boys were pleased with this decision, but my discomfort would not go away.

Then one day at church, someone asked me about jewelry because Seventh-day Adventists discourage wearing it. To explain the reasoning behind this approach to jewelry, I had to work from an underlying principle because the fact is that jewelry taken all by itself is, frankly, a non-issue. Who cares if someone is wearing a small rock or piece of gold or a chain! The problem, I explained, isn't jewelry; the problem is when we are in search of the look-at-me effect.

The apostle Peter, in 1 Peter 3:3, 4, wrote that our adornment should not consist of external stuff but of internal traits. In other words, as a Christian, if people are going to look at me, I need to be sure that the reason they are looking at me is because of what Christ has done in me rather than what I have done to myself. Everyone will freely admit that it is possible to wear accessories that draw attention to all manner of ideas that are less than uplifting. But, by the same token, it is also possible to wear accessories that draw attention to things that *are* uplifting. We must decide what we wear by asking the question, *What will people see when they look at me today?*

After this conversation about jewelry, I got into my truck and suddenly the reason for my discomfort with my truck hit me—it was a different version of jewelry. It was drawing attention to me. Everywhere I went, the topic of conversation was my truck. I came to realize that whenever people saw me, they were not thinking, *There is a great Christian* or *There is a kind person.* They were not even thinking simply, *There is Jeff.* They were thinking, *There is Jeff in his jacked-up truck.*

That is when I knew that in order to avoid being a hypocrite and to be consistent with the underlying principle I had just explained, I had to do something about my own newly purchased look-at-me effect—even if it cost me something to do it. Fortunately, God took over and helped. I'm sure He was involved in connecting me with a person who was selling the same model truck and offered to swap equipment. He removed the lift kit from my truck and put it in his truck, and we traded wheels. It cost me a little—but not nearly as much as it could have. Since then I have not had a single comment about my truck. Evidently, people are seeing just me, un-accessorized, once again. Now I can have conversations that really matter without my vehicle getting in the way.

Doesn't it make sense that a Christian should consider the effect that his or her accessories have on others? And if it seems right to discourage the look-at-me effect in what we wear, shouldn't we, by the same principle, just as enthusiastically discourage look-at-me vehicles, look-at-me homes, look-at-me hairstyles, look-at-me attitudes, look-at-me behaviors, and anything that carries with it the look-at-me effect?

The problem does not lie in our accessories. The problem lies in our desires. What should a Christian hope that others will think about when they see us? The answer to that question will determine the choices we make not just for what we wear and drive but in every situation.

The Lord Is My Shepherd; I Want Bananas

Because memorizing Scripture is difficult work for most adults, I think we underestimate the memorizing abilities of children. From the time they learned to talk, our boys memorized long passages from books we read to them just as easily as the short memory verses we purposely taught them from the weekly Bible lesson. Their brains were like dry sponges thirstily soaking up whatever we fed them.

That fact was sobering, first of all, when we realized that they were repeating more Mother Goose than Jesus and, secondly, because we weren't taking full advantage of this time of easy learning to fill their brains with Scripture. So my wife removed most of the Mother Goose books, and we began reading lengthy Bible passages to see if that might sink into their little heads.

Since sometimes they preferred playing to eating back then, we had to entertain them during meals and feed them while they were distracted. Therefore, mealtimes were great times to teach Bible stories and verses. I started with the Lord's Prayer and soon moved on to Psalm 23 (NKJV). "The LORD is my shepherd; I shall not want." "The LORD is my shepherd; I shall not want," I chanted while serving up broccoli and peas. Quickly, they took up the chant, and so I moved on, "He makes me to lie down in green pastures; He leads me beside the still waters." And so it went. They soaked up the lines effortlessly, unlike me; I have to work hard at it.

But one thing I don't have to work hard at is sloppy interpretation. And, apparently, children are not exempt from the same temptation to cast Scripture in their own image. My son quickly seized upon the idea.

I started the Psalm 23 chant again, and he took over. "The Lord is my shepherd; I want bananas!" he shouted with glee. Trying to stifle my laughter, I started again. He immediately interjected. "He makes me to lie down in green pastures; He leads me—onto the deck!"

Once again, I have learned something of myself and human nature in general from my children. It happens with disturbing frequency these days. Someday I think I'll write a list of everything my kids have taught me about human nature. But to be fair, they have taught me a lot about God as well.

We humans are supremely selfish. Our thoughts swirl continually around ourselves. We work doggedly for our own comfort and gratification, even though we don't know what truly comforts and gratifies.

How often does God promise that we shall not want, yet we work ourselves to death for (or borrow for) what we think we want? How often does God promise to lead us beside still waters, but we decide we would prefer the deck— or the Jacuzzi or the fishing boat?

God's Word is indeed more powerful than any double-edged sword when it's allowed to speak for itself. But when I force it through the filter of my desires, or the filter of my opinions, or the filter of my comfort, I have cast God's Word in my own image, which is merely a form of godliness that denies the power (2 Timothy 3:5).

A Time to Relax and a Time to Rush

Something my wife and I have done every year since our boys were small is that each of us will take one of them for what we call "Boy Days." She takes one boy and I take the other, and we go away overnight on a camping trip or something similar. The next year, we switch boys and do it again.

One year, when my son Erik was about four years old, we went camping at St. Croix State Park in Minnesota. This park was in the district where I pastored three churches. We set up our tent among the trees and then spent the day together randomly doing whatever we felt like doing at the unhurried pace typical of my younger son. For Erik, the task at hand, if it is interesting, is all that is important, and he takes his time doing it. For instance, long after the rest of the family is finished with dessert, he sits at the table slowly savoring every tiny bite. What's next is not something to be considered at that moment. For Erik, there is simply no interest in rushing from thing to thing. What is now is sufficient and should be enjoyed.

After spending the day together at the park, we hiked back to our tent and snuggled into our sleeping bags. Something in the air, though, made me check the weather on my phone. The radar showed heavy storms heading in our direction. Not wanting to overly concern him, I told Erik that it was going to rain, and I hoped we would stay dry. Then we drifted off to sleep. Sometime after 10:00 P.M., I woke up to the sound of a truck-mounted loudspeaker driving through the campground. When it drove close enough to us, I heard the park ranger warning us that the coming storm was dangerous and that we should not remain in our tents. We should move quickly to the storm shelters located in the bathrooms.

I quickly checked my phone again and realized that this could be an all-night ordeal. Waking up Erik, I explained the situation and gave him the choice: Do you want to keep camping here and probably spend the night with lots of other people in the bathrooms, or would you rather go camp in one of our churches that is not too far away?

He pondered the situation with no urgency whatsoever, asking questions about what the bathrooms were like, what would we do for breakfast, and so on. Since I was feeling more urgency than he was, I tried to rush him along in his decision, but he simply would not be hurried. Finally, after the promise of pancakes in the church kitchen the next morning, he opted for camping in the church. He leisurely got dressed while I hastily rolled up sleeping bags. It wasn't raining yet, but the wind was picking up. Erik asked question after question and simply would not concentrate on the task at hand.

Finally, I stopped all of my activity and knelt down in front of him, looked him directly in the eye, and said something along the lines of, "Erik, you need to understand something. Do you see all the people around you madly rushing around? Do you know why they are doing that? It's because there is a really bad storm coming with tornadoes in it. We need to get to shelter quickly. So I need you to stop talking and work fast with me so we can get in the truck and drive away from here."

I didn't actually expect my speech to work, but it did. Erik instantly shut his mouth and began moving faster than I had ever seen him move. I told him to pull tent stakes, and he quickly obeyed. I told him to put sleeping bags in the truck, and he immediately lifted them—even though they were nearly as big as he was—into the truck. Soon we were on the road. Even as we drove, Erik didn't speak. He didn't look afraid, but he looked serious as the storm slammed into us.

At the church, we gathered only what we needed to sleep and ran through the heavy rain into the fellowship hall. I checked my phone again, and the storm did not look as dangerous here as it did at the park. It was nearly midnight. I smiled at Erik as we set up camp in a Sabbath School classroom. "Thank you,"

I said, "for buckling down and helping us get packed up and on the road as quickly as you did. The worst part of the storm is over, so you can relax again."

That was all it took. He relaxed, slowed down, and started asking questions and enjoying the moment again. As we snuggled again into our slightly damp sleeping bags, I finally told Erik that he did need to stop talking and go to sleep now.

What happened that night wasn't something that would normally demand to be remembered, and yet I remember it distinctly. Perhaps it stuck in my mind just so that I could make the connection with what God needs us to do. As the four angels of Revelation 7:1 prepare to release the winds of strife upon the earth, this is no time for the people of God to act as if all is fine with the world. The warnings of Revelation are like God getting down on our level and saying to us, "I need you to understand what is happening here, and I need you to concentrate on what I have asked you to do."

The great controversy between Christ and Satan will be over soon, and then we will have plenty of time to relax and enjoy life.

The Tower

F ive men and I set to work on a project just before Christmas. Our objective was to erect a one-hundred-foot tower on which to mount our radio station antenna.

We waited, stamping our feet to keep warm, until the delivery truck finally found our construction site. When the driver rolled up the rear door, we saw an intimidating array of long, heavy steel pipes, angle iron braces, and a box of hardware that was so heavy that it had to be lifted out of the truck with a forklift.

None of us were experienced tower erectors. In fact, the only reason we were attempting the project in the first place was because the bids we had received from professionals were far above our budget. Our silent question, as we stared at the unassembled tower, was *Can we do this?*

We spread the tower parts out on the ground where someone had cleared a long work area. We ambled around staring at the pieces until the electrician, who was to work on our new church building, arrived. Knowing a good excuse when we saw one, we abandoned the tower to discuss the church's electrical needs.

Meanwhile, Richard arrived. Having not experienced our initial doubts, he boldly approached the box of hardware, opened it up, and extracted the directions. When the rest of us couldn't stall with the electrician any longer, we joined Richard.

We took the directions into the partially completed radio room, found a sawhorse for a table, and spread out the prints. We flipped quickly through the complicated directions without much comprehension—but apparently enough to become dangerous. "Well, let's start," we said.

Abandoning the prints, we strode confidently to the work site and looked again at the intimidating array of pieces. "The largest pipes obviously go on the bottom," we agreed. But which side goes down? They looked the same on both ends. "It probably doesn't matter," suggested someone. (I think it was me.) "It might not matter, but it is worth checking," said someone wiser. We trooped back to our plans but couldn't make sense of them. "Let's call the manufacturer."

I contacted an engineer who informed me that it did, in fact, matter which end went down and it was the end with the stamped numbers. It said so in the directions, he told me. Hoping to prove him wrong, I went back to the prints and sure enough, for someone who was willing to take the time to study them, the directions clearly stated the correct position.

Now we knew positively the way to proceed, so we attacked the project with gusto. Four of us carried the first twenty-foot section of pipe to the foundation but quickly realized that four of us couldn't stand it up. We called all available men working on the construction site to come help. With about eight men, the first pipe was bolted down easily enough. Successful from the first, we went to lunch. Four of us went to Subway.

The Subway group returned first, and so we carried the next pipe to the foundation. The last installation had gone so well that we decided we could do the next one ourselves. We managed not to gash a large hole in the side of the church, but I think it's only because an angel held the top. It was too heavy for us, and we nearly lost it. Wisely, we found more volunteers for the third and final leg of the base.

The first twenty-foot section of the tower was finally bolted together, and the last eighty feet we would assemble on the ground for a crane to lift into place. Feeling like expert tower erectors now, we launched into the next stage of the project, virtually forgetting about the directions.

Someone assumed they were using the proper braces for section two, but after the assembly didn't go well, we went back to the directions. The braces we had used were supposed to go with section three. We disassembled and re-assembled section two. Someone else assumed certain bolts went certain places, but after reading the directions again, we disassembled what we had done and fixed it. I insisted that it did not matter which way the adapters faced on which we were to bolt the final two sections. We wrenched the bolts tightly only to find that the next section didn't fit. The directions showed that they needed to face a certain direction, and we had to redo it.

At the time, someone (I think it was me) said profoundly, "When all else fails, read the directions—but not before." Long ago, someone much wiser said, "There is a way that appears to be right, but in the end it leads to death" (Proverbs 14:12). For pity's sake, read the directions first! That's why God gave us the Bible. Some of the mistakes we make by ignoring those directions cannot be undone.

The Taco Bell Murder

Four young men from my church were returning from a monster-truck event late one night. Caleb was driving. Hungry, they pulled into a Taco Bell drive-through and commenced ordering. Evidently, they didn't order quickly enough for the car behind them, so the driver began to honk his horn and gesture for them to get moving. That probably did not help the ordering process, so it was about five or six minutes before they finally pulled forward to get their food from the window.

After the driver of the car behind them finished ordering, he pulled forward and angrily got out of his car, striding up to Caleb's car and squeezing into the space between the vehicle and the brick wall of Taco Bell. The car's front window didn't work, so Josiah, in the back, rolled down his window. The man shoved his head into the window and began swearing and yelling at the four young men inside, telling them to hurry up. They tried to explain that they were going as quickly as they could. The man ended his tirade by saying that he ought to kill them all right then and there, and then he returned to his car.

Shocked, they couldn't believe that the man was dumb enough to threaten the four of them. What if they were to get out and beat him up in front of his wife or girlfriend or whoever it was that was with him? They didn't seriously consider doing that, however, because they were wise enough to recognize that even if they did beat him up, there would still be consequences for them. "Besides, it wasn't the right thing to do," said Caleb. "Still, we needed to make some sort of a statement."

Suddenly, Caleb knew what that statement should be. "We should pay for his food," he said to the others. "We will kill him with kindness." They didn't know how much it would cost, but they talked it over and decided that is what they would do. Meanwhile, the man continued to blare his horn behind them. When the cashier finally returned with their order, they told him that they were also paying for the car behind them. It turned out to be about ten dollars.

Taking their food, they stopped at the other side of the parking lot to check their orders and prepared to get back on the road. Suddenly, the other car pulled up near them and the man jumped out of his car. Unsure of his intentions, the four young men prepared to get out and defend themselves if it came to that. It didn't. Instead, the man offered his hand and apologized for his behavior and thanked them for their kindness in spite of his rudeness. The four in the car relaxed. "I wanted you to know," said the man, "that I paid for the people behind me." As he walked away, the woman in the other car called out her thanks as well.

Jesus said, "You have heard that it was said, 'Eye for eye, and tooth for tooth.' But I tell you, do not resist an evil person. If anyone slaps you on the right cheek, turn to them the other cheek also" (Matthew 5:38, 39). Jesus knew that repaying evil with kindness is the only fighting technique that will ultimately overcome evil. These four young men experienced the truth of Jesus' command firsthand. That night they fought evil in the most courageous way possible. At a Taco Bell drive-through, they struck a blow that actually murdered evil on the spot.

I will add my thanks to everyone else's for what they did that night. The world is a little bit better place for it. People will be in heaven because of behavior like that.

Goatees and a Worn Bible

Two church members, Mark and Darrell, had joined me at the church to pray. "Let's pray that someone else will join us," I suggested. We did. We prayed that someone would come pray with us, but I suppose we weren't expecting God to answer immediately. Perhaps He would answer the next time we met; perhaps someday in the future. My expectations of God were low—as usual.

Just as we said amen, the outside door slammed and in walked three young men. Sporting goatees, caps, faded jeans, sports shirts, and one worn Bible, the three of them strode confidently into the church basement. Two of them I had never seen; one I had met a couple of times, and he had even come to church once because he had been invited. "I will go pretty much anywhere at least once if I'm invited," he had told me. As they strode in, one pulled an old church bulletin out of his Bible. "It says 'Please come,'" he said, pointing to the announcement for prayer meeting.

"We were just praying that you would come," we told them. "Find a spot." They sat down around our table, and we prayed for another fifteen minutes or so with them and for them. After that, we talked.

I can't relate the entire conversation in these few paragraphs, but the opening remarks were fascinating. One young man was packed full of opinions. "I think

God put everything here on earth for us to use. There is nothing bad if you do it to the glory of God." I looked at Mark and Darrell out of the corner of my eye. They leaned forward as if to say, "Interesting idea. Tell us more." I relaxed. It was a safe place for this young man to talk. And talk he did. They all talked, and so did we. We asked questions. Over the course of the conversation that night, all of us changed our thinking in some significant ways. All of us grew spiritually.

Finally, one of the young men blurted out, "Do you know why people like us don't come to church?" I was all ears. "It's because people automatically condemn us and the way we live without even knowing us. In church, we can't talk like we're talking now."

He was right. I instantly imagined the uncomfortable coughs and squirms I would see in just about any Sabbath (or Sunday) School if these guys were to make their rash statements there, embellished as they were with colorful language. I could imagine the arguments, the offended sensibilities, the defensiveness, and the closed minds. *If I were these guys*, I thought, *I wouldn't come to church either*. "And it's boring," put in another.

But they had not come to complain about church. Church was a non-issue. Church offered nothing for them as far as they were concerned—end of discussion. But they had come to talk about God. They wanted to be heard. They wanted someone to listen and respect their opinion. Once they realized that we respected their opinion, they relaxed and became open to hearing our thoughts as well. These young men were thinkers, striving to be honest in their thinking. All they asked was that we be honest too—honest about our own imperfections, honest about our own limited understanding of God, honest about our own fears, honest about why we live the way we do.

If there is a qualification for growing spiritually, I believe it's a willingness to think honestly. By the same token, if there is a qualification for helping someone else to grow spiritually, I believe it's a willingness to allow someone else to think honestly even when it's diametrically opposed to our sense of right and wrong. Only then can we hope to participate with the Holy Spirit in gently guiding someone's thinking toward the truth as it is in Jesus.

The awesome thing about such conversations is that everyone grows. No authentic spiritual conversation takes place where one person gives everything and the other merely receives. Even a mature Christian has something to learn from a thinker, no matter what he looks like or what he believes, as long as he's an honest thinker and especially when he carries a worn Bible.